ANOTHER WONDERFUL SECRET

INFREQUENTLY ASKED QUESTIONS ABOUT JEFFREY EPSTEIN

GREG OLEAR

Demand me nothing. What you know, you know.
From this time forth I never will speak word.

—IAGO TO OTHELLO IN SHAKESPEARE'S
STAGE PLAY, 1603

———

Happy birthday—and may every day be another wonderful secret.

—DONALD TO JEFFREY IN EPSTEIN'S
BIRTHDAY BOOK, 2003

CONTENTS

AUTHOR'S NOTE

This book is a compilation of a series published at PREVAIL from summer 2025 through spring 2026.[1] The idea was, and still is, to paint as complete a portrait as possible of Jeffrey Epstein as I understand him, based on my years of research.

This is a challenge, because our understanding of him is incomplete. Epstein may be dead, but his story remains a work in progress. There is so much we don't know—and may never know. What we *do* know, meanwhile, is confusing, confounding, contradictory, and, of course, deeply, deeply disturbing.

Many times as I was writing these pieces, I felt like an epidemiologist with a hole in his hazmat suit; I could *feel* the darkness seeping through my pores. But I kept at it. I had to try to understand the pandemic afflicting our society. Is this sickness terminal? If not, how can we recover? Can one be inoculated against it somehow?

As dark and unpleasant as the Epstein saga is, I don't think we can move on as a country until we get to the bottom —that is, to the darkest depths—of it. Epstein was a monster; Donald Trump was his closest friend for decades; we need to know the truth. The future of our democracy—and this sounds like hyperbole, I realize, but it's true—depends on it.

But how, if there's so many blank spaces in the record, can we possibly write a book about Jeffrey Epstein? By asking a lot of questions and answering them the best we can, given the information available to us at the time.

The format of the book, therefore, is Q&A. This format, I think, makes the material easier to digest; provides the widest possible lens through which to observe the totality of the vast, dark forest; and allows me the leeway to address all the speculation—in a story about an enigmatic intelligence guy, there's a lot of that—than would a more "hard journalism" approach. Plus, I get to add a little drollery into what would otherwise be a depressing, dispiriting endeavor. It's written as if you sat down next to me at a cocktail party, and the subject of Epstein came up, and you just kept asking me stuff —and some hostile foreign intelligence service recorded the entire conversation and published the transcript on Wikileaks.

Many of the answers, I will tell you up front, are unsatisfying, or only bring up more questions. That is the nature of Jeffrey Epstein, who in death, as in life, shrouds himself in obliquity.

But that doesn't mean we stop asking.

—G.M.O
New Paltz, NY
May 18, 2026

Voice Over:

There must be more to life than having everything.

Donald

Yes. there is, but I won't tell you what it is.

Jeffrey

Nor will I, since I also know what it is.

Donald

We have certain things in common, Jeffrey.

Jeffrey

Yes, we do, come to think of it.

Donald

Enigmas never age, have you noticed that?

Jeffrey

As a matter of fact, it was clear to me the last time I saw you.

Donald

A pal is a wonderful thing. Happy Birthday—and may every day be another wonderful secret.

Donald J. Trump

CHAPTER 1

THE MONEY THING

. . . I'll pay the cost
For wanting things that can only be found
In the darkness on the edge of town.
—Bruce Springsteen

JEFFREY EPSTEIN IS UNKNOWABLE—BY design.

Unlike the bombastic Robert Maxwell, his model if not his mentor, Epstein kept a low profile. For decades, none of us peasants had ever heard of him—and if we had, he was yet another reclusive "financier," indistinguishable from the other eccentric UHNWIs who live in those Bruce Wayne mansions on Billionaire's Row.

If not for Virginia Guiffre and the other survivors; the indefatigable *Miami Herald* reporter Julie K. Brown; and, of course, Donald Trump (basically the schmuck in *Goodfellas* who after being expressly warned not to flash his money after the Lufthansa heist bought the pink Cadillac and the fur coats), would we even be aware of Epstein's existence?

For decades, the press all but ignored him. There was the

"Bachelor of the Year" snippet in *Cosmopolitan* in 1980 and the Landon Thomas Jr. feature in *New York* magazine in 2002 (Trump: "He's a lot of fun to be with. It is even said that he likes beautiful women as much as I do, and many of them are on the younger side."). Then, a year later, Vicky Ward's "The Talented Mr. Epstein" profile for *Vanity Fair*—shorn, at the eleventh hour, and over her vehement objections, of the bit about Epstein's sexual abuse of the Farmer sisters, ostensibly because her editor didn't think it was "earth-shattering" that Epstein was sexually abusing a 16-year-old.[1]

Aside from the occasional mention in the New York tabloids, usually citing Epstein's proximity to Bill Clinton or Trump, that was about it. There was so little about him in print that the *Palm Beach Post* reporter filing the July 2006 news story about his indictment for solicitation got him mixed up with another Jeffrey Epstein—one who wrote bad checks.[2]

Even now, after God knows how many articles and podcasts and Michael Wolff media hits, what do we really know about Jeffrey Epstein? What can we say for certain?

- For many years, he and Ghislaine Maxwell ran an industrial-scale child sex trafficking operation.
- He was the "closest friend" of Donald Trump, who is currently moving heaven and earth to keep his activities with Epstein under wraps.
- His name was on JPMorgan Chase's "Wall of Cash," because he made the firm so much money.[3]
- There were over a billion dollars' worth of suspicious transactions on his accounts at JPMorgan Chase—and that was only one of the banks he regularly used.
- Dozens upon dozens of rich and powerful people— among them Larry Summers, Alan Dershowitz, Bill Gates, Peter Thiel, Elon Musk, Steve Bannon,

Kathryn Ruemmler, Howard Lutnick, Leon Black, Ehud Barak, Ian Osborne, John Brockman, Jes Staley, and Woody Allen—remained in contact with him, well after his monstrous sex crimes became impossible to claim ignorance of.

- Most of the rich and famous people in his orbit did *not* participate in sex crimes—as far as we know.

The child sex trafficking operation is so abominable, so unthinkably awful—and, critically, so well documented by the accounts of so many survivors—that it demands the lion's share of the media's attention. And rightly so. Release the files! Expose every last one of those monsters!

But for Epstein—and this is painful to write and ugly to contemplate—the sex trafficking was a sideline from his core business. Because there's one more thing we know for certain about Jeffrey Epstein:

- Sometime between 1981, when he left Bear Stearns, and 1991, when he joined forces with Ghislaine Maxwell, Epstein went from being a *rich* dude to a *wealthy* dude. He leveled up.

Graydon Carter, Vicky Ward's then-editor at *Vanity Fair*, justified the excision of the Farmer sex abuse allegations in that 2003 feature by telling her, "I think the money thing is more interesting."

The money thing is not more interesting. The money thing, on the contrary, is intentionally boring. Half the reason offshores are so hard to unravel is because tracking shell company upon shell company upon shell company in tax haven upon tax haven upon tax haven is mind-numbingly dull. As the economic sociologist Brooke Harrington reports in *Offshore: Stealth Wealth and the New Colonialism*, "Even those who do specialize in this system sometimes use the term MEGO (My Eyes Glazeth Over) to describe it."

So no, the money thing is not more interesting. But it *is* more important to understanding what Jeffrey Epstein really was.

———

So what was he?

In a word, indispensable. Not to you and me and the other hoi polloi, and certainly not to the victims of his odious crimes. But to the "power elite," Jeffrey Epstein was indispensable.

We know this for certain, because even when it became clear that he was a pedophile and a child sex trafficker, his rich and powerful friends basically shrugged and kept right on talking to him like nothing had happened.

Why was he indispensable?

For starters, people—many people; many rich and powerful people—clearly enjoyed his company and valued his advice. We see that in the emails released by his estate. But that isn't what made him indispensable.

Jeffrey Epstein did three things better than anyone else.

First off, he was one of the best in the world at using offshores to safeguard the fortunes of the wealthy. He hid money. Or, to be more precise, he employed "tax avoidance strategies," in which the objective was to shield his clients' fortunes from taxation.

Second, he was a power broker—a connector. He connected dangerously powerful people to other dangerously powerful people. He was a prominent figure in the shadowy worlds of state intelligence services and arms dealing—and equally prominent in the no less shadowy worlds of politics, high finance, academia, and technology. He knew people, and he knew people who knew people. And everyone took his calls.

Finally, to those cohorts who shared his deviant predilections, Jeffrey Epstein was a Charon who ferried the rich and the powerful, the brilliant and the influential, across the River Styx, away from polite society and into the darkest reaches of Hades.

So: Epstein could help you evade the tax man; introduce you to a former Israeli prime minister, or an AI pioneer at MIT, or the CEO of The Limited, or David Copperfield; and, if you're a sicko pervert like him, procure a fifteen-year-old for you to rape, without having to worry about the consequences.

Plenty of people could help you take advantage of the lax tax laws in the Bailiwick of Jersey. Very few could call up a member of the British royal family if something went awry there. And if you add in what I will euphemistically call "massage?"

Only Jeffrey Epstein could do that.

How did a nobody from a middle-class family in Queens make himself so indispensable to so many rich and powerful people?

From his days as a teacher at the hoity-toity Dalton School, Epstein was exposed to wealthy people, so he knew the big secret. The wealthy, as Harrington explains in *Offshore*, "don't manage their own money. Many, like the parents of [a] chewing-gum heiress I met at summer camp, didn't even know how to change their own lightbulbs. They had housekeepers and other 'staff' to handle the daily challenges the rest of us face ourselves. Do-it-yourself financial management was out of the question for most of them—particularly because their fortunes were multigenerational, usually transnational, and far too complex for any one person to grow and protect."[4]

Epstein wanted to be a guy who grew and protected those multigenerational, transnational, and complex fortunes. That was the goal. So he leveraged a connection at Dalton to land a job at Bear Stearns, where he specialized in a gray area of finance—"taxation strategies"—that would eventually land him on the wrong side of the SEC. And he leveraged *that* arcane knowledge to ingratiate himself to rich and powerful people in England.

England? Why England?

Because that's where fate took him. In 1981, Epstein visited London with his then-girlfriend, Paula Heil Fisher. At the time, she worked at Bear Stearns, the brokerage firm Epstein had recently parted ways with (at least officially).

It was on that trip to London that Fisher introduced Epstein to Nick Leese, whom she'd met previously at a shindig in Houston. Nick's father was Douglas Leese, whom Epstein was also introduced to while he was in town.

This was *the* key relationship in Epstein's origin story. No Douglas Leese, no Jeffrey Epstein.

What was the nature of Epstein's relationship with Douglas Leese?

As *The Sunday Times* reports,[5]

Epstein was "mentored" in the early 1980s by Douglas Leese, a British former arms dealer, and eased into establishment circles by members of Oxford's infamous Bullingdon Club, including his eldest son, Nick.

The arms dealer "immediately saw promise in Epstein," as his son Julian recalled for *The Times*:[6]

> In his only interview with a journalist before his death from cancer last year, Julian Leese said: "Dad understood, 'Here was a very intelligent person who was very clever with the stock market' and he gave Dad some advice. Dad was enamoured with Jeffrey and Jeffrey was enamoured with Dad as a sort of mentor.
>
> "You have to remember something about Jeffrey: in those days, he was 27, he was amazingly charismatic and great fun … The whole family liked him and he would come down on many occasions to our family home in Wiltshire."

Let me get this straight—Epstein was "mentored" by a British arms dealer?

According to no less an authority than *The Times*, yes.

Why don't we ever hear about Douglas Leese?

Because he's been dead for almost 15 years. And even when he was alive, he didn't have much of a digital footprint. There's more pictures online of J.D. Salinger than there are of Douglas Leese.

I'm intrigued. Who is Douglas Leese, exactly?

A "flamboyant" businessman—wealthy enough to have his own fifteenth-century country house, South Wraxall Manor, which is now owned by John Taylor, the heartthrob bassist of Duran Duran.

Back in the day, *The Times* tells us, Leese hobnobbed with Donald and Ivana Trump's bosom chum Adnan Khashoggi, the billionaire Saudi arms dealer...[Leese's] name later surfaced in parliament in connection with the record Al-Yamamah contract for the sale of British fighter jets to the Royal Saudi Air Force. Douglas Leese was accused of handling secret commissions on behalf of British Aerospace through an offshore bank.

A filing from a separate court case in the U.S. stated: "The nature and extent of Leese's activities, and his various contacts around the world, involve highly sensitive and confidential information, some of which are believed to be classified by the Department of Defense and other agencies of the United States government."[7]

It was around this time—that is, the mid-1980s—that Epstein began telling people he worked in intelligence.

Did *Leese* work in intelligence?
We can't say for sure. Under British law, Leese would not have been allowed to say if he worked for MI6.

However, Steven Hoffenberg—the fraudster who in 1987 hired Epstein to run his Ponzi scheme operation at Towers Financial, and who served 18 years in federal prison—claimed, after his release, that Leese had recruited Epstein to work for British intelligence.

Hoffenberg's entire business plan was founded on lies, so take what he says with a grain of salt. But if it's true...I mean, why would a guy recruit someone to work for British intelligence if he didn't work for British intelligence himself?

Bigger picture, it seems unlikely that the British government would outsource the brokerage of a major arms deal with Saudi Arabia to a British national who *didn't* work for the Secret Intelligence Service.

· · ·

Was *Epstein* involved with those big arms deals?

Well, Epstein was working for Douglas Leese, and Douglas Leese was involved with the arms deals. What else would Epstein be doing? Leese didn't pay him all that money to iron his shirts.

For a more detailed answer, I defer to the intelligence analyst Thomas Hampson:[8]

> Yet another indicator that intelligence agencies favored Epstein was the false passport found in his New York mansion when it was searched in 2019, which he apparently kept as a souvenir since it had expired (in addition to being fake). The fake Austrian passport showed Epstein under a different name and with an address in Saudi Arabia. Entrance and exit stamps indicate that the passport was used in the early 1980s and was used in locations that parallel those used to facilitate the Al-Yamamah arms deal.
>
> I can't imagine Epstein getting a fake passport or using one without official government backing and cover. Intelligence services made counterfeit passports.

Court documents are more explicit about this, refuting Epstein's claim that he never traveled with the fake passport, only keeping it to show "potential kidnappers, hijackers, or terrorists" while traveling in the Middle East, to conceal his Jewish surname. "In fact, the passport contains numerous ingress and egress stamps, including stamps that reflect use of the passport to enter France, Spain, the United Kingdom, and Saudi Arabia in the 1980s."[9]

In the Reagan/Thatcher era, the world was not exactly awash with arms dealers reliable enough to broker the Al-Yamamah and Iran-Contra deals. Deals of that size and magnitude required a very specific skill set.

Leese was involved. Khashoggi was involved. Manucher

Ghorbanifar, an Iranian arms dealer, is said to have come up with the underlying concept of Iran-Contra.

Why would the arms dealers need Jeffrey Epstein?
Because, as we discussed, Epstein could do one thing better than almost anyone else: hide money. That's what he specialized in at Bear Stearns. That's why Ace Greenberg kept him around even after his dust-up with the SEC.

Both Al-Yamamah and Iran-Contra required vast sums of money to move around without detection. At the time, Epstein may well have been the best man in the world at doing that work who *wasn't* an organized crime figure.

Too, Leese was "accused of handling secret commissions on behalf of British Aerospace through an offshore bank," per *The Times*, which, if true, smacks of Epstein's involvement.

Could fees from these arms deals have been the initial source of Epstein's wealth?
Put it this way: Adnan Khashoggi did not become the richest man in the world by selling ladies' underwear.

But Leese and Epstein had a falling out.
Leese sacked Epstein after he busted him expensing Concorde flights and five-star hotels to his company's account. Or so the story goes.

"So the story goes?" You don't think that's true?
No.

Why not?

Because I don't think Epstein would have jeopardized his relationship with Leese like that. Nor do I think Leese would have cared that much about Epstein turning in a gaudy expense report.

Furthermore, Epstein was still friendly enough with Nick Leese that in 2003, Leese wrote a rather naughty note in the "birthday book"—a distasteful vignette involving his father (called "Doggie"), a Filipino friend of his named Toto, and a woman who was either a high-priced escort, Leese's mistress, or both:

You very dear boy,
····· Going back into the past as I have over the last few days has in some ways prooved a melancholy experience all the old criminals suddenly came leaping out at me Mac,Ogilvy,Swire,Baring,Alfonse, the Brigadier,the old man and all the good times that we had together.One of the sad things in life is that fate conspires to move people apart to the extent that I hardly see you any more but,I suppose that is why we are compensated by memories.
······ I was speaking to BB last night before writing this e-mail and we both agreed that we were at a loss to decide which of the hundreds of hilarious incidents to pinpoint for you,there are just too many.Inspecting the Royal School girls dorms,chasing rabbits with Toto in the old mans dino,trying to get█████husband out of the way in Manila,blocking Ogilvies loo with the illegal goose at Barings wedding ,doing three point turns in the tunnel in HK when we asked the Mandarin driver to find us some girls,dancing the night away in the Tin Mine in KL,massage classes at Wraxall.....and so on and so on it brings tears to my eyes.
·· However, there was one evening which I recall always had you howling with laughter.We were in Harry's Bar in London you ,me ,the old man ,Toto,█████ and the usual extraordinary group of camp followers Lord Long,Ian Cruikshank,etc etc.Somehow Toto got it into his head that █████was a call girl that doggie had fixed up for him.after dinner we all went off to Tramps and Toto and doggie got into the back of doggies car with █████sitting between

Finally, it was Leese who recommended Epstein to his next employer, the aforementioned Steven Hoffenberg. According to Hoffenberg, Leese told him Epstein was brilliant and "had no moral compass."

That doesn't sound like a "falling out" to me. That sounds like an amicable divorce—or else a cover story for a relationship that never ended. But that's just me speculating. I have no way of knowing for sure.

It *is* true that while he was working for Leese, Epstein was also taking on private clients. Turns out, he was not only good at hiding money; he was also good at finding it.

Finding it?

Yes. In the late 80s, Epstein billed himself as a sort of financial bounty hunter.

Did he have any notable clients?

He did indeed! The private investigator Hampson explains:

> While all this was going on, Epstein was hired by the famous Spanish actress **Ana Obregón** to recover millions of dollars of her father's money that had been lost. Obregón's father, **Antonio Garcia Fernández**, had invested heavily in **Drysdale Government Securities**. The firm collapsed in May 1982 due to fraudulent bond practices. Drysdale's failure triggered a $300 million loss, putting Fernández's entire holdings in jeopardy.
>
> To pursue the recovery of Obregón's money, Epstein hired **Robert A. Gold**, a former **Assistant U.S. Attorney of the Southern District of New York,** to partner with him. Gold specialized in securities law, and he had contacts in the Southern District of New York, which was prosecuting the Drysdale fraud. Epstein, using his research abilities, leveraging his contacts, and with the help of Gold and his contacts, the 29-year-old Epstein [sic] engineered the recovery of millions of Obregón's money.
>
> So at the same time the young Epstein was impressing MI6, the CIA, the Israelis, and everybody else involved in the nefarious transactions that facilitated Al-Yamamah and Iran-Contra arms sales, he was dazzling his famous and very well connected client Ana Obregón, and earning the respect of

seasoned attorneys like Gold and of the prosecutors in the Southern District of New York.[10]

Whoa—that's a lot of intelligence agencies!

And it's not even a complete list. You can add Saudi intelligence, because of those arms deals, and, almost certainly, the KGB as well.

Wait—wasn't Alex Acosta, the U.S. Attorney who brokered the ridiculous 2008 non-prosecution agreement, told to lay off Epstein because he "belonged to intelligence?"

That's the word on the street, although Acosta remains cagey about the whole thing.

He was deposed recently, as part of House Oversight's Epstein investigation. It's a disappointing transcript. Unless my search function is not working properly, not once in the deposition does anyone so much as utter the word "intelligence." So we still don't know *if* anyone actually told Acosta that—and if someone did, we don't know who it was.[*]

Furthermore, the phrase "belongs to intelligence" doesn't tell us which country's intelligence agency Epstein might have belonged to.

Is that last sentence a joke?

Only if you think it's funny.

The Israelis were involved in Iran-Contra?

---

[*] Alan Dershowitz said something on a podcast recently suggesting that he was the one who said that to Acosta, but who knows.

Intimately. Brown University's "Understanding the Iran-Contra Affairs" website offers a helpful explainer:[11]

> In 1985, Ghorbanifar and [Adnan] Khashoggi came into contact in Hamburg, Germany, and began devising the skeletons of the plan that would eventually become the Iran side of the Iran/Contra Affairs. Three Israelis were drawn into the discussion in the summer of 1985. A number of stories exist regarding the exact time, place, and specifics of these meetings. However, from these meetings came the idea to sell U.S. arms to Iran via Israel and the suggestion that, to gain the U.S.'s approval for the scheme, American hostages in Lebanon could be released. At the same time this was happening, the NSC was searching for new ways to deal with Iran.

If Epstein was involved with Iran-Contra, he must have been liaising with Israeli intelligence—specifically, the Military Intelligence Directorate, or AMAN. That's the intelligence arm of the IDF.

[pause]

Aren't you going to ask me who the head of AMAN was from 1983-85?

Okay, I'll bite. Who was the head of AMAN from 1983-1985?
Ehud Barak.

The former Prime Minister?
Bingo! Barak looks like a poli-sci professor now, but he was a badass who served for decades in the IDF.

He and Epstein invested in an Israeli start-up company in 2015, after he left public service. In 2023, *The Times of Israel* reported:[12]

According to the WSJ's Wednesday report on the calendar's contents, Barak visited Epstein about 30 times between 2013 and 2017 at his estates in Florida and New York, including a time in 2014 when the former Israeli premier flew with Epstein on his private aircraft from Palm Beach to Tampa, after which Epstein went on to New York. Barak said his wife and an Israeli security guard were also on that flight. He said he flew with Epstein on his private plans on one other occasion, also with his wife and guards.

According to the report, Barak also met with Epstein monthly for nearly a year, beginning in December 2015.

The meetings came well after Epstein's 2008-2009 conviction and sentencing for procuring a child for prostitution, but Barak has maintained that he had no knowledge of Epstein's activities.

Raise your hand if you believe that a former head of state *who used to run an Israeli intelligence agency*, and who visited Epstein 30 times *after* the 2008 non-prosecution agreement, had no idea what his buddy was doing with all the girls.

Didn't Virginia Guiffre mention…

A "former Prime Minister" who was so violent with her that she was afraid she might not survive the encounter? A sadist she was so frightened of she declined to name, for fear of reprisal?

She does, on page 360 of *Nobody's Girl*:[13]

> our abusers, we also must protect ourselves. You may notice that while
> I've named some men in this book, I have not named all the men I was
> trafficked to. Partly that is because I still don't know some of their
> names. Partly, too, that is because there are certain men who I fear
> naming. The man who brutally raped me toward the end of my time
> with Epstein and Maxwell, for example—the man whom I've called
> "the former Prime Minister" in court documents—I know his name,
> and he knows what he did to me, even though when others have sought
> comment from him about my allegations, he has denied them. I fear
> that this man will seek to hurt me if I say his name here.

Do you think…?

I'm not saying a word, or implying anything! Barak said
he had no idea what Epstein was up to with the girls, and
what possible incentive would he have to lie?

I *will* point out that Barak lost re-election in 2001, where-
upon he reportedly came to the United States to work for
Electronic Data Systems. Guiffre was with Epstein from 2000
until 2002, and traveled around with him extensively.

But that doesn't mean Barak is the "former Prime Minister" Guiffre was talking about! There were probably scores of
"former Prime Ministers" in Epstein's inner circle!

Scores **of "former Prime Ministers?" Like who? Name one.**

Like…um…uh…

You know what? Let's just move on—or, rather, move *back*,
to the mid-80s.

You see, there was another notable figure Epstein reportedly did work for at that time. Hampson, the private investigator, explains:

While Epstein was working with Douglas Leese and Adnan Khashoggi, he was introduced to **Robert Maxwell**. Epstein reportedly helped Maxwell recover and restructure assets tied to Maxwell's publishing empire, including offshore trusts in Liechtenstein and the Channel Islands.

You really think Epstein knew Robert Maxwell in the 80s?
Absolutely.

Robert Maxwell inserted himself in the middle of everything, and played the various intelligence agencies—MI6, Mossad, the CIA, and the KGB—off one another. That was his game. He swam in the same pool with Khashoggi and the other arms dealers. He was also, through his activities with the Russian mob boss Semion Mogilevich in Communist Bulgaria, a pioneer in offshores and money laundering.

In the 80s, Epstein was working for a British arms dealer who allegedly recruited him for MI6. His specialty, as we have seen, was offshores—the exact same financial shenanigans Maxwell was involved with.

How many people were cavorting with arms dealers *and* British intelligence *and* setting up offshores in the 1980s? A dozen? *Two* dozen? What are the chances that their paths never crossed?

Think of it this way: A major league baseball team has 26 players on its active roster. Robert Maxwell and Jeffrey Epstein not knowing each other in 1985 is about as likely as Babe Ruth and Lou Gehrig not knowing each other in 1927.

Not only that, but I believe Robert Maxwell was the template for what Epstein wanted to become.

But Ghislaine Maxwell told Todd Blanche that her father never knew Epstein.

That's right, she did. She also said that *she* met Epstein for the first time in 1991:

```
            GHISLAINE MAXWELL:   I met Mr. Epstein in

1991.  My -- I had -- I had never heard of him or met

him before.  And no one in my family had ever either.

My father never knew him.  And I'll explain why that

is the case. I met --
```

And you think Ghislaine's lying?

It is my personal opinion that she is full of shit, yes.

Yeah, but, I mean, she would remember when she met Epstein for the first time.

This is a woman who *routinely* committed perjury. Routinely.

We've already discussed how her father and Epstein must have known each other. So that bit about her dad not knowing Epstein seems to me to be a lie—and one she offered up herself, without prompting.

Now, the Jeffrey/Ghislaine *relationship* may have started in 1991. But I believe—and again, this is just my opinion—that they met previously.

Why do you think Ghislaine and Jeffrey met prior to 1991?

Because Epstein's old Bear Stearns crony Elliot Wolk said so in the "birthday book:"

> Jeffrey I remember in the mid 1970s you being a star salesman for our tax advantaged strategies and hedged option program. I was running an account for Bob Maxwell. You always had the ability to know everyone and be charming. Was that when you first discovered the Maxwell teen-age daughter.......Happy Birthday Elliot Wolk

That note—which was written in 2003, when no one involved thought this would matter at all two-plus decades in the future, and therefore had no reason to lie—strongly suggests a mutual familiarity with Robert Maxwell, and implies that Epstein made the acquaintance of "the Maxwell teen-age daughter" *long* before 1991.

You said something before about the Channel Islands. What are the Channel Islands?

Channel, as in English Channel. Islands, as in an archipelago off the coast of France. These are the islands William the Conqueror, the Duke of Normandy, brought with him when he invaded England in 1066.

Jersey and Guernsey are the two important ones—the Crown Dependencies.

What is a Crown Dependency?

One of three island territories—the Isle of Man is the third—ruled by the King but not formally part of the United Kingdom.

Jersey, in particular, is a notorious hotbed of financial chicanery—one of the first places in the world to actively cultivate offshore business.

Stuart Syvret, a native of Jersey and a former Senator there, who ran afoul of the ruling elites when he dared to investigate a child sex scandal, describes the political system on the island as an absolute monarchy. As I wrote back in 2021, when I had him as a guest on the PREVAIL podcast:

> Syvret was responsible for Jersey's equivalent of Child Protective Services. It was in that post, while filling those responsibilities, that he became aware of a rampant child sex scandal involving the island's orphanages. He spoke out about the horrific abuses he'd uncovered—and was promptly silenced by the Senate. Rather than confront a problem as ugly as it was insidious, Jersey's ruling elites bent over backwards to cover up the scandal, going so far as to have Syvret arrested, three times, on cooked-up charges. Unlike political prisoners anywhere else in the Western world, Syvret was denied legal representation.[14]

There's so much money sloshing through the system there that Jersey is nicknamed "the Trillion Dollar Island." As I wrote five years ago, back when Charles III was still the Prince of Wales:

> Blended in with outsized corporate earnings, the filthy lucre of IRS-averse billionaires, and dirty rubles sloshing in from Russia, is the wealth of the royal family. The Queen's personal bank, Coutts, has an active branch in Jersey. So does Deutsche Bank. It's quite the mix.

So: Jersey is

1. home to a gigantic child sex scandal involving friends of the royal family,
2. a notorious tax haven where all manner of shady individuals park their money, and
3. the site of a branch of an underhanded bank that recently paid a *$75 million settlement* to the sex abuse survivors.

It has Jeffrey Epstein's name written all over it.

Wait—the Queen was involved in this?

She had a small fortune parked offshore; her name appears in the Panama Papers. Although I highly doubt she was *directly* involved.[15]

Then who *was* directly involved?

I can't say for certain, but for ten years, from 2001-2011, the Special Representative for International Trade and Investment for UK Trade & Investment was a chap named Andrew Mountbatten-Windsor.

Who?

Prince Andrew.

You mean…?

Yes.

Do we know what Epstein really thought of Prince Andrew?

The Canadian journalist Ian Halperin says that Epstein told him that "[t]he royal family were 'completely brilliant' because they were the 'richest motherfuckers' in the world, while collecting money from British taxpayers," *The Times* reports.

The British historian Andrew Lownie, author of *Entitled: The Rise and Fall of the House of York*, said that Prince Andrew "was easy prey for a rattlesnake like Epstein." Epstein, Lownie wrote, "played Andrew. The prince was a useful idiot who gave him respectability, access to political leaders and business opportunities. He found him easy to exploit."[16]

So the Duke of York was played by the Dude from New York?

I guess? The thing is, ~~Prince Andrew~~ Andrew Mountbatten-Windsor has been living high on the hog, well above his means, for decades now. As Rob Evans of *The Guardian* wrote in October:[17]

> How on earth does Prince Andrew fund his lifestyle?
>
> This is a man who has lived a life of luxury for decades, been an outcast for years because of his association with Jeffrey Epstein, yet has no visible means of financial support.
>
> Even King Charles is said to be unsure about some of the sources of his brother's income, particularly how he finds the significant sums of money needed to afford the upkeep of his home, the 30-room Royal Lodge.
>
> The disgraced prince has been able to keep his financial affairs from the public for years through a mixture of the traditional secrecy which envelops the Windsors and the confidentiality of his dealings with wealthy, mainly foreign, people.

In addition to Jeffrey Epstein, those "wealthy, mainly foreign, people" include a Libyan warlord, a Tunisian despot, a well-heeled relative of a Kazakh strongman, and the autocratic president of Azerbaijan.

So in the Andy/Jeffrey relationship, I'm not sure who was "playing" whom. I don't think Andy is some rube—or a useful idiot, tempting as it is to cast the world's sweatiest nepo baby in that light. He may not have had his finger on the pulse of the common man, but he knew what was going down with his mommy's money.

. . .

Why do you say that?

Back in 2008, while his buddy Epstein was in hot water in Palm Beach, Andrew went to some international business function and behaved like a total…can I say the c-word if I'm describing a British guy? Better not risk it…he behaved like a total dick.

According to a secret cable written by the U.S. Ambassador to Kyrgyzstan, and released via Wikileaks, the Prince "railed at British anticorruption investigators, who had had the 'idiocy' of almost scuttling the Al-Yamama [sic] deal with Saudi Arabia."[18]

This was in reference to "an investigation," the cable says, "subsequently closed, into alleged kickbacks a senior Saudi royal had received in exchange for the multi-year, lucrative BAE Systems contract to provide equipment and training to Saudi security forces."

And then: "His mother's subjects seated around the table roared their approval. He then went on to [denounce] 'these (expletive) journalists, especially from the National [sic] Guardian, who poke their noses everywhere' and (presumably) make it harder for British businessmen to do business. The crowd practically clapped."

BAE Systems? What's that?

That's the company formed by British Aerospace after a 1999 merger.

Hang on…wasn't Douglas Leese "accused of handling secret commissions on behalf of British Aerospace through an offshore bank?"

Yes. Yes, he was.

· · ·

Was Prince Andrew also involved with that?

I have no idea. But that's pretty clearly what he was referencing at that business event.

When did Epstein and Prince Andrew meet?

In 1999, via Ghislaine Maxwell—supposedly. *She's* known Andy her whole life, pretty much.

Supposedly?

It's certainly possible, as Andrew wasn't a key player in the Crown's finances until 2001. Even so, I don't necessarily trust the "official" timelines.

Epstein told Halperin, the Canadian journalist, that he'd met Queen Elizabeth and introduced Princess Diana to Dodi Fayed. Those grandiose claims seem ridiculous at first blush, until we recall that Epstein was helping Douglas Leese move money around during Al-Yamamah, and also allegedly setting up offshores in Jersey and Guernsey for Robert Maxwell. Plus, Dodi Fayed was the nephew of Adnan Khashoggi, Epstein's acquaintance and, allegedly, one of his clients.

Epstein was a legendary bullshitter, to be sure. But it's not impossible.

And we know Robert Maxwell was on friendly terms with Queen Elizabeth.

Correct. There are pictures of them together from the 70s and 80s. He's actually touching her.[19]

· · ·

How did Robert Maxwell meet, and become friendly with, the Queen?

No one knows. I just read an extremely well-sourced and riveting book by Gordon Thomas and Martin Dillon called *Robert Maxwell, Israel's Superspy: The Life and Murder of a Media Mogul*. There's all kinds of great material in that book. But not once do they mention Maxwell's relationship with the Queen. Most curious.[20]

Had Epstein met Les Wexner by the end of the 80s?

Yes. As Wexner himself recalls:[21]

> I first met Mr. Epstein in the mid-1980s, through friends who vouched for and recommended him as a knowledgeable financial professional. Mr. Epstein represented that he had various well-known and respected individuals both as his financial clients and in his inner circle. Based on positive reports from several friends, and on my initial dealings with him, I believed I could trust him.
>
> Eventually, he took over managing my personal finances. He was given power of attorney as is common in that context, and he had wide latitude to act on my behalf with respect to my personal finances while I focused on building my company and undertaking philanthropic efforts.

But that doesn't mean Wexner "made" him. Not at all. I get that the Victoria's Secret magnate has long been pegged as the original source of Epstein's wealth. But the truth is, Epstein was *already* rich and extremely well-connected *before* he started working for Les Wexner.

Is Wexner correct when he says granting power of attorney is common in that kind of arrangement?

As I understand it—with the caveat that this is not my area of expertise—yes.

Remember what Brooke Harrington writes in *Offshore*: the ultra-wealthy don't do anything for themselves—*especially* manage their vast fortunes. People are baffled by the POA thing, but I think it's one of the least weird things about Jeffrey Epstein. Wexner is worth something like $9 billion. He didn't need to manage it all himself; it's not like he was going to go broke. He wanted to focus on other things, which I totally understand.

People are also baffled at why Wexner—and, later, Leon Black—kept Epstein on for so long, even after it became dodgy to do so. Harrington has an answer for this, too:

> Many of the ultra-wealthy harbor politically sensitive, potentially explosive secrets of a financial, legal, and personal nature. As one Swiss wealth manager I interviewed put it, clients must metaphorically "undress in front of you," because all their most private information affects their fortunes and the legal-financial strategies needed to protect them. Finding wealth managers who can be trusted with such information is a lengthy and fraught process. Another wealth manager I interviewed recounted, "One of my client said to me after years working with him, 'You know I can't sack you now. You know where everything is, you know everything about me.'" ….
>
> In the world of offshore finance, trust is not a commodity and cannot be purchased easily from another provider.

So once you decide on a wealth manager…
It's easier to divorce your wife than fire them.

. . .

When did Wexner give Epstein power of attorney?

In 1991.

Huh. Nineteen ninety-one seems like a big year in this story.

Yes. In 1991 Robert Maxwell falls—or has his corpulent corpse pushed—off his yacht, the *Lady Ghislaine*. The actual Lady Ghislaine shows up to meet the press, tells them she thinks her father was murdered. Then she relocates to NYC, where she takes up with Epstein, whom Wexner has just given power of attorney. (He's not living in Wexner's mansion yet; he's renting out the old Iranian Embassy.)

That year also marks the end of a chapter.

The end of a chapter?

For a long time, Epstein maintained "normal" romantic relationships. He dated Eva Anderson, the Swedish model, off and on for 11 years in the 1980s—and he was friends with her for years after they broke up, even after she married his pal Glenn Dubin.

With that said, he was always a creep, always had a perverted attraction to girls, and was allegedly abusing women as early as 1985. He was accused of sexually abusing a 13-year-old girl in 1990.[22]

But the child sex *trafficking*? That didn't begin until Ghislaine Maxwell came along.

There were other changes, too, as the private investigator Hampson lays out:[23]

When Ghislaine became involved with Epstein, there was a dramatic shift in Epstein's method of operation. He changed:

- from attending parties to hosting them

- from being exclusively involved in relationships with adult women to recruiting young girls for sexual purposes
- from having no training for any of his staff to becoming a facilitator orchestrating the grooming and training of underage girls, and girls barely of age, to become sexual companions of powerful men, similar to the training described in the Kama Sutra
- from having no surveillance cameras on his properties to having multiple hidden cameras, including in bedrooms and bathrooms

But the big one—let me reiterate—is this: *there's no evidence of Epstein engaging in child sex trafficking before he teamed up with Ghislaine.*

Oh man. This has my head spinning.
MEGO, my friend. MEGO.

MEGO?
My Eyes Glazeth Over.

CHAPTER 2
COMMODITY FLOW INFORMATION

> *"...dark men in mien and movement, flashing in their mocking mirrors the obscure soul of the world, a darkness shining in brightness which brightness could not comprehend."*
> —James Joyce, *Ulysses*

———

ARE we sure Epstein was a creep before Ghislaine came along?

Here is an anecdote related by the late Jesse Kornbluth, the prolific *Vanity Fair* writer and author, that speaks to Epstein's personality:[1]

> When we met in 1986, Epstein's double identity intrigued me —he said he didn't just manage money for clients with mega-fortunes, he was also a high-level bounty hunter. Sometimes, he told me, he worked for governments to recover money looted by African dictators. Other times those dictators hired him to help them hide their stolen money. . . .
>
> My wife-to-be was then a military historian, with a book about to be published. *Interview Magazine* photographed her

in a buttoned-up military shirt, with a taut khaki tie. A witty photo of an attractive woman. But not a sexy look. Jeffrey Epstein had chatted her up at a few parties. The military look fooled him not at all.

The night before our marriage, Epstein called. "It's your last free night," he told my wife-to-be. "Why don't you come over and fuck me?"

That was how, in June of 1987, Jeffrey Epstein became dead to me.

Unseemly. Disrespectful. Creepy. But par for the course, for the predatory rich guy set. And: does not involve raping children.

What about Ghislaine?

Well, Virginia Guiffre said Ghislaine—or "GMax," as she calls herself—was a bigger monster than Epstein. Have you read Guiffre's book? Or the indictment?[2]

What was Ghislaine...sorry, *GMax*...like before she met Epstein?

For some insight into Ghislaine's non-child-sex-trafficking behavior, here is another anecdote from Jesse Kornbluth:

In the early '90s, at a Joan Rivers dinner party, my wife and I encountered Ghislaine Maxwell, daughter of disgraced British publishing mogul Robert Maxwell and Epstein's girl-friend for a brief period in the '90s....I'd met her several times with Epstein; we were also "friends," in that transac-tional Manhattan way. And might now become better friends. "If you lose 10 pounds, I'll fuck you," she said, with my wife standing next to me. And she too became dead to me.[3]

I also have it on good authority that, like Epstein, Ghislaine is a big starfucker—constantly bragging about her father (objectively, a massive piece of shit) and namedropping all the famous people she knows. Even to the trafficked girls, she bragged. She once told Virginia Guiffre that at some random party, she gave George Clooney a blowjob.

Is that true?

Clooney vehemently denies it, Ghislaine is a fabulist and a perjurer, and it's not like she ever anticipated Virginia would grow up to publicly call bullshit on her claim. So: probably not.

I mention it not to sully poor George, but to give an example of her shameless namedropping.

[beat]

What is it? What's on your mind?

Just that, after all this time, I still don't really understand the nature of the relationship between Jeffrey and Ghislaine.

No one really does. It just brings up more questions.

Was she the Radar to his Major Burns, or was it the other way around? Did they really *both* get off on what they were doing? Were they ever actually in love? Were either of them capable of love?

In many ways, the pair of pervert predators seemed like an old married couple. Organizing the "birthday book" for his fiftieth, for example, is the sort of thoughtful thing a wife does for a husband (or vice versa). But Epstein had other girlfriends subsequently, which didn't seem to faze her in the slightest—and at the time of her arrest, Ghislaine was married to, or at least nuptially involved with, a fellow named Scott Borgerson.

. . .

Who?

Scott Borgerson. I wrote about him in 2020—before a lot of the legacy media:*

> Married or not, Borgerson and Maxwell did have some kind of relationship—a romantic one, if the tabloids can be trusted The *Daily Mail* reported that "Borgerson, 43, the CEO of a tech company, left his wife, Rebecca, for the 57-year-old five years ago, a source close to the family said," and that "Maxwell had been living with Borgerson at his $3m oceanfront mansion in Manchester-by-the-Sea for the past three years." Manchester-by-the-Sea is in Massachusetts, north of Boston —less than two hours away from Tuckedaway, the New Hampshire redoubt where Maxwell was busted by the FBI.
>
> The *Daily Mail* presents a less-than-flattering portrait of Scott Borgerson: he left his wife and kids to be with Ghislaine, but before he left, there was a history of (alleged) heavy drinking and (alleged) domestic abuse. According to the divorce papers, he once threatened his wife: "Don't make me beat you in front of the kids."
>
> So Ghislaine's knight in shining armor is not exactly Tom Hanks. But then, this is not the romance of the century. There are compelling reasons why Borgerson would be attracted to Maxwell, and vice versa—and none of them have anything to do with love.

A former Coast Guard officer, Borgerson was the CEO of CargoMetrics, a tech company that "applies big data to the shipping lines," as I wrote. His enterprise was

---

* Shout out to Rachel Slade.

billed as a "maritime innovation company," and it is. As I understand it, the company's proprietary software aims to monitor not just where the ships all are—via their AIS, or automatic identification system—but where they've been, and, ultimately, what they're carrying. This would make it possible to have a granular overview of the entire world's ocean transport system.

Yeah, but, as you said, that was six years ago. Where's Borgerson now?

He stepped down as CEO of CargoMetrics a few weeks after Ghislaine's July 2020 indictment, and he very gallantly dumped her for a younger woman as soon as she went to prison—or so I have read.

As for the financials, that is more interesting. Felix Yim writes at *BBN Times*:[4]

Scott Borgerson's net worth is estimated to be around $20 million to $25 million as of 2025, primarily derived from his role as the co-founder and former CEO of CargoMetrics, a Boston-based data analytics company focused on maritime trade and shipping. Founded in 2010, CargoMetrics was valued at approximately $100 million in 2020, reflecting its innovative approach to leveraging big data for global shipping insights. Borgerson's wealth was bolstered by his leadership in securing high-profile investors, including Google's Eric Schmidt and billionaire hedge-fund manager Paul Tudor Jones, connections reportedly facilitated through Maxwell's elite social network. His financial portfolio also includes significant real estate holdings, such as a $2.4 million ocean-front mansion in Manchester-by-the-Sea, Massachusetts, and a $1 million property in Bradford, New Hampshire, purchased in 2019 under a shell company, where Maxwell was later arrested.

Borgerson's financial dealings with Maxwell further complicate his net worth. In 2016, Maxwell reportedly transferred the majority of her estimated $20.2 million fortune into a trust controlled by Borgerson, a move that surfaced during her 2020 bail application. This trust, combined with their joint assets, was cited in a $22.5 million bail package, including $8 million in property and $500,000 in cash, underscoring their intertwined finances.

Yim also notes, "His denial of a romantic relationship with Maxwell, despite evidence of cohabitation and shared assets, has fueled speculation about his motives and credibility."

Like I said, not exactly the romance of the century. If anything, it reads more like an arranged marriage from the High Middle Ages.

Paul Tudor Jones? That sounds like a lost member of Spinal Tap. Who's he?

Yet another billionaire hedge fund guy. Made his fortune predicting the Black Monday market crash of 1987—the original Big Short. (He was in his 30s at the time, and, per *Institutional Investor*, "develop[ed] a reputation for courting models and partying long into the night.") Was buddies with [*checks notes*] Harvey Weinstein. Now lives in Palm Beach. Started the Robin Hood Foundation, a poverty-fighting charity, with Epstein buddy Glenn Dubin. One of his daughters is a country singer who plays in the Zac Brown Band.*

Important to stress that he's never been accused of

---

* The Zac Brown Band, FWIW, is billed as the musical headliner for UFC Freedom 250, the caged fighting match scheduled for Trump's 80th birthday on the White House South Lawn.

anything untoward, and there's no reason to think he ever will be.

There seems to be no shortage of hedge fund guys.

Alas, yes.

How has CargoMetrics fared since GMax went to Supermax?

From what I can tell, the company is doing well. It rebranded, invented some stuff, took on partnerships with big multinationals. I'd invest in it, if I were a billionaire; unlike a lot of AI, it actually does something useful.

The first patent it filed after Borgerson stepped down involves a "system and method for generating commodity flow information."[5] It looks pretty cool:

Patent number: 12001992

Abstract: Disclosed is method including receiving digital vehicle data for a fleet of vehicles like trucks, trains, planes, drones, etc., the digital vehicle data being one or more of GPS/location-based data, image data or radar data and combining one or more of pieces of data. The method includes inferring, based on the first combined data or based on incomplete data, a loaded/empty status of a vehicle. The method includes combining other data to yield second combined data, receiving data regarding one or more of supply, demand, and amount of available cargo to yield third combined data, generating information relating to a supply of vehicles available to load at a specified dock and/or deliver a cargo to a specified dock, in each case within a specified period of time and generating suggestions for one or more vehicles regarding future routes based on the data.

Type: Grant

Filed: March 22, 2021
Date of Patent: June 4, 2024
Assignee: CARGOMETRICS TECHNOLOGIES, LLC
Inventors: Scott G. Borgerson, James E. Scully, Ethan E. Rowe, Robert A. Weisenseel, Ronnie Hoogerwerf

Make of that what you will.

Why would Ghislaine Maxwell be interested in maritime trade routes?

As I speculated in the piece,

> Per CargoMetrics, seaborne cargo transports some $9 trillion of goods per year—90 percent of all the things that go from Point A to Point B. Of all of that, Customs inspects a vanishingly small percentage. Most stuff gets where it's going, no matter what it might contain. The software Borgerson's developing could help crack down on smugglers and criminals—or it might do the opposite. If I'm a big fish in a global crime syndicate, I'd love to have a clearer understanding of global shipping. That would make it easier for me to move my banknotes, my arms, my drugs, my gems, my sex slaves, to avoid detection by authorities. To be clear: there's no indication Borgerson has this in mind —other than the fact that he courted "oligarchs" as investors.

Also, GMax has a submarine pilot license. And apparently she enjoys the sea. Maybe it makes her feel closer to her dad?

Ouch!

Too soon?

Speaking of Robert Maxwell—if Ghislaine has some financial stake in CargoMetrics, it would not be the first time that a

Maxwell family member made money from cutting-edge computer software that would be of interest to foreign intelligence agencies, organized crime syndicates, and terrorist groups.

Oh?

As Gordon Thomas and Martin Dillon extensively cover in *Robert Maxwell: Israel's Superspy*, her father, Robert Maxwell, was the exclusive salesman for PROMIS, a cutting-edge spy software. This represented a sizable chunk of his income during the 1980s, the authors suggest.

Originally developed in the 70s for the Justice Department to integrate cases in the byzantine U.S. legal system, the software was purloined by Mossad, souped up, repurposed, fitted with a "backdoor," and made available to Maxwell's various and sundry contacts in the foreign intelligence services. In time, *all* of those spy networks ran PROMIS. (Mustn't have a Cutting-Edge Spy Software Gap!)

But Robert Maxwell didn't limit himself to spooks. As Thomas and Dillon explain,

> In October 2001, a month after the destruction of the Twin Towers in New York and the attack on the Pentagon in Washington by al-Qaeda suicide bombers, it emerged that the man who controlled them, Osama bin Laden, had acquired a copy of the still highly secret PROMIS software.
>
> The version of PROMIS provided to bin Laden came from a former FBI agent, Robert Hanssen. For years he had been a Russian spy inside the FBI. He had passed over the latest version of PROMIS to his handlers in Moscow. They had sold on a copy to Simeon Mogilevich for a reputed sum of $3 million. He had sold it on to bin Laden for an undisclosed price.

. . .

Who is Semion Mogilevich?

He is—or perhaps *was*; he's long in the tooth now, assuming he's still alive—the head of the Russian mob, with deep ties to the KGB and, more recently, to Vladimir Putin. Citjourno found footage of him at a Putin campaign event in 2000.[6]

Get right out of town!

That's apparently how the U.S. tracked down Bin Laden: via Felix Sater, the former Trump business associate who apparently leveraged his contacts in the Russian underworld to locate the al-Qaeda leader. He claims to have been a Confidential Informant, and the former Attorney General Loretta Lynch not only confirmed this, but credited Sater with being instrumental in finding UBL.[7]

But Robert Maxwell died in 1991; Osama Bin Laden was killed in 2011. Why would Russian mobsters know his whereabouts, two full decades later?

Maybe Osama and Semion were in the same "FBI Most Wanted" fantasy football league? I don't know, and I'd rather not speculate.

Wasn't Robert Hanssen Opus Dei?

I'm reluctant to claim that anyone "is" Opus Dei. What we *can* say is that Hanssen was part of a small circle of D.C. insiders under the sway of the Rev. C. John McCloskey III, an Opus Dei priest who ran the Catholic Information Center.

. . .

Who else was in that small circle?

Sam Alito; Clarence and Ginni Thomas; dark money maestro Leonard Leo; the late columnist Robert Novak, who outed Valerie Plame as a CIA operative; Louis Freeh, the former FBI Director who later, as a private attorney, took on Prince Bandar bin Sultan of Saudi Arabia as a client for legal proceedings involving the Al-Yamamah arms deal we discussed in Chapter One; and, oh yeah, Bill Barr.[8]

Bill Barr Bill Barr?

The same.

[pause]

I can see that look in your eye. Settle down, Alex Jones. Please, I implore you: *don't* jump to any conclusions here.

D.C. is a small city. People know each other. Just because people encounter each other socially, or go to the same church, or follow the teachings of the same radical Catholic priest who was accused by a parishioner of sexual improprieties, doesn't necessarily have any larger significance. Certainly it doesn't prove the existence of a secret cabal hell-bent on world domination.

You're no fun.

It's like when random people turn up in pictures with Maria Butina or Ghislaine Maxwell—those two actively collected photos of themselves with important people. All it means is that they were once in the same place at the same time.

At Little St. James, Epstein displayed a framed photo of him and GMax meeting Pope John Paul II. That doesn't mean the Catholic Church was involved in child sex trafficking.

Okay, bad example. Moving on…

•   •   •

Speaking of people appearing in photos with Ghislaine— why is no one talking about how Melania Trump fits into all this Epstein stuff?

Because she sues anyone who brings it up.

Back in August 2025, in a piece about the once and current First Lady, I wrote about the myriad unanswered questions about Melania Trump vis à vis Epstein:

What was *her* relationship like with Jeffrey Epstein and Ghislaine Maxwell? Melania has been with Donald since 1998; Trump didn't break with Epstein until late 2004. She's front and center in the most widely circulated photo of Donald, Jeffrey, and Ghislaine. Epstein told the journalist Michael Wolff that he was Trump's closest friend for ten years and that "the first time [Donald] slept with [Melania] was on my plane." [9] If true—and I'm not inclined to believe a word that came out of that self-aggrandizing monster's mouth, but he *did* make the claim—that suggests a level of comfort between Melania and Epstein. How well did *she* know him? When did *they* meet? Why would Epstein have claimed that he introduced Donald to Melania, if the couple met via Paolo Zampolli? [10] Did *she* spend time at his house in Palm Beach or his mansion in New York? Was *she* ever with Epstein and/or Maxwell without her husband? Was she asked to do stuff? Did *she* have any interaction at all with the girls on Epstein's properties? Was *she* aware of Epstein's pedophiliac predilections? Was it possible for her *not* to be aware, given Donald's 2002 "It is even said that he likes beautiful women as much as I do, and many of them are on the younger side" quote in *New York* magazine? If so, why didn't she do anything about it? Virginia Guiffre was working at the spa at Mar-a-Lago when Ghislaine Maxwell "recruited" her in 2000, shortly after Melania was photographed at a tennis-tournament party there with Trump, Epstein, Maxwell, *and* Prince Andrew; was Melania aware of *that*? Did she know Virginia in 2000? Did she encounter Virginia subsequent to her leaving Mar-a-Lago?[11]

Is *she* in the Epstein files?

These questions, alas, remain unanswered.

Why don't more journalists dig into this?
Like I said, fear of litigation. Remember, Melania threatened to sue Hunter Biden *for quoting Epstein talking about her.* Legacy media has legal departments begging them to steer clear.

But also, it's hard work. Mary Jordan, author of the Melania biography *The Art of Her Deal: The Untold Story of Melania Trump*, wrote about the challenges she encountered while researching her subject:[12]

> Finding out more about Melania—her past, her motivations, her daily life—has been an unprecedented challenge. In three decades as a correspondent working all over the world, I have often written about the reluctant and the reclusive, including the head of a Mexican drug cartel and a Japanese princess, but nothing compared to trying to understand Melania. Most people I spoke to would not speak on the record. Many in the Trump world are governed by NDAs (nondisclosure agreements). Some had been warned by lawyers, family members, and others close to Melania not to speak publicly about her, and many would talk only on the same encrypted phone apps used by spies and others in the intelligence community. Old photos that were once an easy Google search away no longer pop up online.

The journalist and author Nina Burleigh had a similar experience doing interviews for her book on the Trump women, writing, "Anyone who has tried to learn what

Melania Knauss was up to in the years between leaving Slovenia around 1990 and washing up in New York City a few years before she says she met Trump in 1998, finds a lacuna, a blank slate on which there is almost no record."[13]

This sort of opacity is what we might expect from, say, an arms dealer like Douglas Leese. But a FLOTUS? We know more about Lucretia Garfield than we know about Melania Trump.

So you're saying this is unusual?

That is my opinion, yes.

At the time, Melania was a recent arrival from Eastern Europe.

She was. She came here, she says, in 1996, and according to MAGA lore and her own autobiography/coffee table book, first met Trump in 1998.

And Melania wasn't alone. Lots of women were arriving in the U.S. and Western Europe in the mid 90s from the newly-ex-Communist countries behind the Iron Curtain.

"Arriving?"

I didn't want to write "being trafficked" and "Melania" in the same sentence, because I don't want to imply or suggest or insinuate anything that might rouse her attorneys.

Let me be clear: Melania came to New York with Paolo Zampolli on August 27, 1996! Of her own volition! There are documents to prove this! For a few years in the mid 90s, she even lived within walking distance of my Manhattan apartment!

．　．　．

But girls *were* being trafficked from Eastern Europe in the early 90s.

Sadly, yes.

As Gail Kligman, a professor of Sociology and Director Designate of the Center for European and Eurasian Studies at UCLA, noted in a talk in 2005:[14]

> The collapse of communism that began in 1989 provided new resources—geographical and human—for the sex trade, increasingly incorporating women from Eastern Europe. One of the most striking images of the changes soon after the fall of the Berlin Wall was that of women lining the highways offering sex for sale. Political and economic liberalization as well as internal and international militarism created new opportunity structures and daunting economic uncertainties that produced both a demand for and a supply of sex workers in and from Eastern Europe. Most of these sex workers have been and are women and girls.

Robert Maxwell was, per *Superspy*, an avid customer in the Bulgarian sex trade on his frequent visits to Sofia. As I mentioned, one of his business partners in the years before his death in 1991 was Semion Mogilevich—who, as the FBI explains (boldface mine),[15]

> has been a transnational organized crime boss active for many years operating from Russia and various other countries. In 1995, the Russian Ministry of the Interior (MVD) identified Mogilevich as the boss of more than 300 criminal associates operating in more than thirty countries in Europe, Asia, and North America. Mogilevich's criminal organization engaged in a wide variety of criminal activity, included murder, extortion, **trafficking in women for prostitution,** weapons trafficking, money laundering, bank and securities

fraud, and, in numerous countries, the corruption of public officials.

Was Robert Maxwell's involvement with Eastern European prostitutes not confined to his own personal pleasure? Was he also part of the Mogilevich sex trafficking operation? And if so, was his (hypothetical) stake in that sex trafficking operation Ghislaine's *real* inheritance?

In other words, was the Epstein/GMax sex trafficking operation just an extension of a potential Mogilevich/RMax sex trafficking operation? And if so, might *that* have been a major source of Epstein's income?

Because, again: *there's no evidence of Epstein engaging in child sex trafficking before he teamed up with Ghislaine.*

I thought most of the Epstein survivors were girls he and Ghislaine recruited from the Palm Beach area.

That's true. But we have to keep one thing in mind: JPMorgan Chase reported—belatedly—over a *billion* dollars in suspicious transactions across Epstein's accounts. Many of these were cash withdrawals, believed to be used to pay off the girls he trafficked and to otherwise finance that operation.

That's *significantly* more cash than necessary to fund his own illicit activities with the survivors he and Ghislaine recruited locally; heck, it's enough to give a thousand bucks to every resident of Palm Beach County! The staggering amount of money suggests that the sex trafficking was on a much larger scale than, and was not limited to, the girls he and GMax abused personally.

Furthermore, JPMorgan Chase was just *one* of the four big banks he regularly used. The real sum total of those suspicious transactions might approach two billion dollars.

• • •

That's a lot of money.

It's more than the national debt of Afghanistan.

As Nina Burleigh points out over at the indispensable *American Freakshow*,[16] there's enough about "Epstein's known communications with pals, his flight logs, and scheduling emails with staff" in the public domain to get a sense of the scale of his trafficking operation:

Between 2013 and 2019, Epstein frequently flew unnamed women to and from East European airports—Kyiv, Moscow, Yekaterinburg, and Warsaw—as well as Stockholm and Helsinki commercially through Paris.

These trips almost always include [redacted] passengers —nameless individuals whose screening in the documents suggests they are trafficked victims whose names are purposely shielded.

Burleigh continues:

The scheduling emails are but a tiny keyhole glimpse into Epstein's activities. As we previously reported, Epstein made 64 unexplained voyages through the Istanbul airport between 2010 and 2014, at a time when global watchdog groups were reporting a surge in human trafficking through that city in the wake of the Middle Eastern refugee crisis.

This new cache of scheduling emails suggests that he engaged in trafficking through Paris with [redacted] passengers right up until his arrest at Teterboro—on a return flight from France—in 2019.

Why Paris? You don't hear that much about his residence there.

For one thing, Epstein used it as his European hub. Burleigh explains:

> Epstein's playmates in Paris included Fiat heir and mega-industrialist Eduardo Teodorani and Hermes billionaire Axel Dumas. Epstein dined with Norwegian diplomat and Oslo Accords hero Terje Rød-Larsen (who took Epstein money for a Greek island pad and visited his NYC mansion numerous times) and even hosted a three-day overnight stay at his Avenue Foch apartment for the Secretary General of the European Council, Norwegian politician Thorbjørn Jagland, during the 2015 Paris Fashion Week.

More importantly, Paris is one of the modeling capitals of the world. And the promise of a modeling career was one of the ways he lured unsuspecting girls into his dastardly clutches.

Remember, Epstein bankrolled the 2004 creation of MC2 Model Management, the agency run by the French national and notorious sex creep Jean-Luc Brunel—who, incidentally, was *also* found dead in his prison cell of apparent suicide.[17]

Brunel met Epstein through Ghislaine, whom he'd known since the 1980s—another indication that she was the prime mover of the sex trafficking.

Wasn't it Brunel's modeling agency that repped Ivanka Trump, during her days as a teenage model?

No—but I understand your confusion. That was *another* pedophile modeling agent Trump was pals with: John Casablancas.

His reputation as a creeper was well known *long* before Donald allowed his fifteen-year-old daughter to work with Casablancas's Elite Modeling Agency in the mid-90s. In the mid-*80s*, Casablancas got divorced for the second time after having a public affair with the model Stephanie Seymour, whom he started "dating" when she was 14.

Oh dear God.
Well put.

Wasn't Elite the premier modeling agency at the time?
It was. In fact, Casablancas played a big part in making "supermodels" a thing. Elite's clients included Cindy Crawford, Linda Evangelista, Claudia Schiffer, and Naomi Campbell.

Naomi Campbell—she was close with Epstein, right?
She's certainly in a lot of photos with him—candid photos, not the kind Maria Butina took. And her entry in the "black book" contains several addresses and a dozen phone numbers.

Did they meet through Casablancas?
I don't know. More likely, they met through Les Wexner, the head of Victoria's Secret and Epstein's client.
(Although she was never an "Angel," Naomi Campbell walked the second Victoria's Secret Fashion Show and was associated with the brand.)

Brunel was also arrested on sex trafficking charges, and also "committed suicide" while in custody.
Yes.

. . .

He also hanged himself in his prison cell.

That's what the coroner's report says.

Come on, dude.

What?

Two pedos, both part of the same sex trafficking network, both arrested around the same time, both committing suicide in their prison cell, both dying the same way.

Yes, and?

You don't think that's fishy?

It's certainly a remarkable coincidence.

For real? You really think Epstein offed himself? You're really buying that? Really?

I find it perfectly feasible that he would do that, yes. But honestly, I don't care. I'm just glad he's dead.

But Donald Barr, Bill's old man who used to work for the OSS, hired Epstein when he was headmaster at Dalton! And he wrote that creepy sci-fi book about teenage sex slaves! And Bill Barr, who _used to work for the CIA_, personally visited the prison right before he died!

Stop. Just stop.

Donald Barr and Bill Barr were both involved with U.S. intelligence at some point in their careers, sure, but what does that prove?

The former headmaster may have hired Jeffrey originally —no one can say for sure—but he retired the semester before

Epstein started teaching there. There's no evidence they even spoke after that one interview.

Don Barr writing some lousy sci-fi novel that *might* have appealed to Epstein—Was Epstein a reader? Was there even a single book at any of his residences?—means nothing beyond the fact that two men who worked at a fancy coed prep school were eying little girls with bad intent.

As for the rumor that Barr visited Epstein at the Metropolitan Correctional Center, that has been debunked.[18] The newspaper that originally published the claim retracted the story. The only source was some second-rate mobster, a convicted perjurer who wasn't even in New York when Epstein was in jail.

But *Bill Barr* was in New York when Epstein was in jail!

That's true. Per Factcheck.org:[19]

> Barr did happen to be in New York City on July 23, speaking at a cyber security conference, the day after Epstein reportedly was found injured in his cell and put on suicide watch. But there is no evidence that Barr paid a visit to the Manhattan prison.

It proves zilch. Bill Barr is *from* NYC. He grew up there, went to high school there, and then went to Columbia. It's not like he randomly flew to OKC or Florence, South Carolina. It isn't at all unusual that he would make a trip to his hometown—especially when his hometown is New York Fucking City.

Barr was recently deposed about Epstein's death. I read that transcript, hoping for some clues. But, while I don't exactly trust him, nothing he said about the death rang false to me.

. . .

But there are so many irregularities around Epstein's death!

There are also indications that he killed himself, such as him changing his will right before he died.

He might have done that because he knew the *kidon* was coming to get him!

All the conspiracy theory fodder—the video not working, the guards not checking in, him not being on suicide watch, etc.—could much more easily have been arranged by Epstein himself than some covert Mossad kill team. I mean, he was *there.*

And *so many people* had a motive! Trump, the Clintons, the British royal family, the Israelis, the Russians, Harvard, any number of tech bros...

Someone call Benoit Blanc! This could be a *Knives Out* movie!

With that said...there *is* one little detail I noticed that caught my attention.

Oh?

After Epstein's July 2019 indictment and arrest, Les Wexner came under a lot of scrutiny. He was, for a long time, Epstein's only known client, and there was the unusual arrangement about the power of attorney that we already talked about—"inexplicable" was the word the papers usually used to describe it. I'm sure Wexner was sick of people asking about it. Probably he was embarrassed; nobody likes to be made a fool of.

On July 16, 2019, Wexner put out a statement about Epstein, via the Wexner Foundation:[20]

I would never have guessed that a person I employed more than a decade ago could have caused such pain to so many people. My heart goes out to each and every person who has been hurt. I severed all ties with Mr. Epstein nearly 12 years ago. I would not have continued to work with any individual capable of such egregious, sickening behavior as has been reported about him. As you can imagine, this past week I have searched my soul ... reflected ... and regretted that my path ever crossed his.

When Mr. Epstein was my personal money manager, he was involved in many aspects of my financial life. But let me assure you that I was NEVER aware of the illegal activity charged in the indictment.

We all know that what is being reported about Mr. Epstein will receive significant news coverage. I fully expect that this will remain in the news for some time to come. And we don't know what twists and turns these events will take ... but I can assure you that I will continue to act in the company's best interest as this unfolds, and I ask you to do the same. I am proud that our company has long-held core values—those values have never been more important than today, and I ask that we all wave them higher now than ever before.

A few weeks later, after mostly staying out of the spotlight, Wexner issued another, longer statement.[21] This was after he'd accused Epstein of "misappropriating" tens of millions of dollars:[22]

In recent weeks, there has been considerable media attention on my past connection to Jeffrey Epstein. To be clear, I never would have imagined that a person I employed more than a decade ago could have caused so much pain. I condemn his abhorrent behavior in the strongest possible terms and am sickened by the revelations I have read over the past weeks. I sincerely value your trust, and that is why it is important you hear details and context from me directly.

I first met Mr. Epstein in the mid-1980s, through friends who vouched for and recommended him as a knowledgeable financial professional. Mr. Epstein represented that he had various well-known and respected individuals both as his financial clients and in his inner circle. Based on positive reports from several friends, and on my initial dealings with him, I believed I could trust him.

Eventually, he took over managing my personal finances. He was given power of attorney as is common in that context, and he had wide latitude to act on my behalf with respect to my personal finances while I focused on building my company and undertaking philanthropic efforts.

In the early 1990s Mr. Epstein became a trustee of The Wexner Foundation, but he had no executive responsibilities in the running of the Foundation. He did not work directly with Foundation staff, and he did not engage with leadership initiatives in any way.

As the allegations against Mr. Epstein in Florida were emerging, he vehemently denied them. But by early fall 2007, it was agreed that he should step back from the management of our personal finances. In that process, we discovered that he had misappropriated vast sums of money from me and my family. This was, frankly, a tremendous shock, even though it clearly pales in comparison to the unthinkable allegations against him now.

With his credibility and our trust in him destroyed, we immediately severed ties with him. We were able to recover some of the funds. The widely reported payments Mr. Epstein made to the charitable fund represented a portion of the returned monies. All of that money—every dollar of it—was originally Wexner family money.

I am embarrassed that, like so many others, I was deceived by Mr. Epstein. I know now that my trust in him was grossly misplaced and I deeply regret having ever crossed his path.

As the story has unfolded further, and the extent of the pain caused by Mr. Epstein continues to grow, I have spent time reflecting and searching for answers as to how this could have happened. My heart goes out to each person who has suffered unthinkable pain and I pray for their healing.

That's a thoughtful, honest, and compassionate statement.

Yes. Nice work by Mr. Wexner.

Why are you bringing it up?

Because it was sent to the press on Wednesday, August 7, 2019, and posted to the Wexner Foundation website on Thursday, August 8, 2019.

So?

Epstein was found dead first thing in the morning on Saturday, August 10, 2019. Which means he probably died the night of Friday, August 9.

Which means…

Wexner releases that statement on a Wednesday afternoon; Epstein's dead before sunrise on Saturday.

Are you saying…?

No! No, no, no, no, *no!*

Let me be *very* clear: I'm not accusing Wexner of anything. There wasn't even that much time between the two statements—roughly the amount of time it might take to get together with a crisis PR team and craft a longer statement. It's not like he had Epstein's date of death circled on his calendar as some sort of deadline (no pun intended). And it was a *few days* later, not *the same* day.

Plus, who would Les Wexner dispatch to MCC to do the hit—lingerie models with angel wings? Please. I'm quite sure it was a coincidence.

Then why bring it up at all?

Because the timing struck me as odd. Compiling my notes, I went back and checked the dates. I assumed that the second Wexner statement would have come right *after* Epstein's death. Instead it was exactly the opposite. It came right *before*. A weird coincidence that I wanted to flag.

Again—I am making no accusations, and I don't want to suggest or even *imply* that Wexner did anything wrong or was involved in any way. I am quite sure he was not.

But if this *were* a Benoit Blanc movie, I mean, that would be a wild plot twist, right?

Knives Out: Victoria's Secret **would be the working title.**

Brilliant! Have Rian Johnson give me a call.

We're getting off track again.

It comes with the territory.

Do we know where Epstein's head was at before he got arrested?

On June 1, 2019—about six weeks before his arrest—a few people sent Epstein the link to a short news story in *The*

Hill about the attorney Emmet Flood leaving the White House.[23]

Michael Wolff quipped: "Now look what you've done."

Nicholas Ribis, who was once CEO of Trump Hotels & Casino Resorts, was more serious: "They r all jumping ship - its totally crazy - it's time to worry."

"Time to worry?" Worry about what?

I don't know. But Flood's departure was clearly of interest to Epstein—or so his friends thought.

Flood was Trump's attorney when the Mueller Report dropped. Donald tweeted: "[Flood] has done an outstanding job – NO COLLUSION – NO OBSTRUCTION! Case Closed! Emmet is my friend, and I thank him for the GREAT JOB he has done."

The *New York Times* wrote this:[24]

The arrival of Mr. Flood, who previously worked at the firm Williams & Connolly and last worked in the White House Counsel's Office under George W. Bush, signaled a more emboldened front as the investigation dragged on. As Mr. Mueller's office weighed the possibility of issuing a subpoena against Mr. Trump, Mr. Flood was among several lawyers who quietly worked to curtail access to the president. In the end, Mr. Trump never sat for an interview with Mr. Mueller.

It just struck me as strange that, of all the things happening at that time, Flood leaving a job everyone expected him to leave was given so much attention.

Anything else of note about the Epstein emails?

Epstein seemed to have had an inordinate amount of

engagement with Steve Bannon. He was supposed to have breakfast with Bannon the day after his arrest, according to the emails.

What was Bannon up to?

He was making a documentary about Epstein. There's even a trailer for it on YouTube. The objective, ostensibly, was to help Epstein rehabilitate his image.

Why would Bannon do such a thing?

As a challenge? To see if he could?

I haven't a clue. Of all the characters in this ten-year Trump saga, Steve Bannon is the most inscrutable to me. I can't figure him out. Although, to be fair, I don't have any desire to.

Didn't Epstein make him a list or something?

Yes. In one of the last dispatches before his arrest, Epstein writes himself a note, subject heading "list for bannon steve," that reads like a passage from James Joyce's *Ulysses*:[25]

mandelson, barnaby summers watson, axel bottstein. karim terje, pritzker edelman. set lloyd, martin novak minsky, tata susskind, strominger krauss, hopkins. randall, kosslyn, gardner gates, thiel. hoffman, hoie sinofsky, sheldrake, suzlberger. jes staley, joscha bach, joi ito. HBJ berge, miro, anas raafat, sultan, nathan feigenbaum, ramashandran, goelberg. demasio, shristakas brockman hillis, kaufman, seligman. gould, saks, john kery, george mitchell, mandelbbrot. chomsky, barrack barak, zagat, nathan, brian greene, yau, eo wilson, prince andrews, jagland, clinton pastrana, richardson, leahy, jarecki, schumer, ranieri, waheed, mongolia, gambat ehud, jacque lang woody, churkin, sergey, ruemmler, weingarten, amabani, rochsild, dersh, ken starrk karp,, dubai castro, pople queen, pres king pm, mandelson balir, , mette, , midlefafrt; gergen,. melusine margarita ovitz. barrak, mabuto, kashoogi, rockefeller,

What the fuck does *that* mean?

Frankly, I'm more qualified to analyze the Joyce. But let's examine the text, shall we?

It looks like it was typed out manually—probably dictated to someone who couldn't type fast enough to keep up and/or was unfamiliar with the names. One of his Russian admins, perhaps?Voice-to-text wouldn't screw up the spellings that badly, and I doubt that Epstein would himself type out "rochsild" for Rothschild.

We see a lot of familiar names (Prince Andrew, Bill Clinton, Larry Summers, Bill Richardson, George Mitchell, Woody Allen) on the list; a lot of lawyers (Alan Dershowitz, Ken Starr, Reed Weingarten, Kathryn Ruemmler, whose surname is spelled correctly); a lot of billionaires, including ones from the Middle East (HBJ is Hamad bin Jassim bin Jaber Al Thani, the former Prime Minister of Qatar; "Waheed" is presumably Al Waleed bin Talal Al Saud, the wealthy Saudi royal who was arrested during MBS's Kushner-assisted purge in 2017); bankers (Jes Staley), academics (Noam Chomsky), AI gurus (Marvin Minsky, Stephen Kosslyn), titans of Silicon Valley (Bill Gates, Peter Thiel, Reid Hoffman, Alex Karp), and assorted Norwegians (Terje Rød-Larsen, Thorbjørn Jagland, Celina Midelfart); and, towards the end, a series of titles: pope, queen, president, king, prime minister. Ehud Barak and Peter Mandelson are listed more than once.

It can't be a guest list, because there are people mentioned who are no longer alive (Mobutu Sese Seko, Fidel Castro,

Vitaly Churkin, Minsky, Richardson, both of the famous Khashoggis). It can't be a kompromat roster, because his attorneys wouldn't be on a list like that—and neither would the Pope. "Dubai" and "Mongolia" are names of places, not people.

Why *this* list for Steve Bannon? Was it part of the documentary project? A money map, as co-host Stephanie Koff theorized on *The Five 8*? Or is it something completely innocuous—all the people he has pictures of him shaking hands with, say?

Like the Nighttown section of *Ulysses*, I don't know what it means.

Hang on—why is Schumer's name on the list?

You tell me. I'm also curious why "suzlberger" appears. Sulzberger is the name of the family that publishes the *New York Times*, the paper of record that has routinely crapped the bed these last nine years.

What's more notable, however, is the obvious omission.

Donald Trump?

Bingo.

How *does* Donald Trump fit into all this?

That's the million-dollar question—the answer to which Trump has gone to extraordinary lengths to conceal.

Something I have observed: No one's talking about the nature of the relationship between Ghislaine Maxwell and Donald Trump. We hear about Ghislaine and Jeffrey, we hear about Jeffrey and Donald, but we never hear about Donald and Ghislaine.

Trump hates women and is routinely nasty to women he

doesn't like, as the White House press corps can confirm. But he's always been deferential to GMax. The only other person he treats like that is Putin. He's just *itching* to commute her sentence, you can tell.

Why would he do that?

To buy her silence.

Her silence *about what?*

[sighs]

We already know Trump is a serial sexual assailant. We know he's an adjudicated rapist. We know he's a felon, convicted on 34 counts. We know he's a Kremlin stooge. We know he launders money for the Russian mob. We know he comes from the world of organized crime. We know he's a rat.

We know he was best buddies with Epstein for at least a decade and a half—that he partied with him and shared an interest in underaged girls. We know he allowed Epstein and GMax to "steal"—his word—girls from Mar-a-Lago for them to traffic and rape.

We know all of that already. None of it has moved the needle. *Part of the White House* has fallen, but Trump remains.

We also know that whatever's in the Epstein files is very very *very* bad—worse than any of the stuff we *already* know. That's been trickling out in reporting by David Shuster and Allison Gill, among others.

We know there's a push within the Bureau to disclose what's in those files. We know this because Jason Leopold's FOIA request about the FBI's review and redaction of the Epstein files was cranked out in *record* time; it can take many months, and sometimes years, to get replies to FOIA requests, and many of them bring back little of value. Leopold got this one back in a matter of weeks, and it was enlightening.[26]

Finally, we know that Donald Trump never wants the Epstein files to see the light of day. He's genuinely terrified that what's contained there will end his presidency. Why else would his lickspittle Kash Patel authorize $851,344 in overtime for FBI agents to redact *Donald's name* from the documents?

So the question we have to ask ourselves is, hypothetically speaking, what could possibly be worse—I mean, like, *orders of magnitude* more damning—than what we *already* know? Because what we already know is awful.

I'll bite. What could possibly be worse—hypothetically speaking—than all of that?

Your guess is as good as mine. I do have some thoughts on what would be worse. Hypothetically speaking. What would make even the staunchest MAGA turn on him. Stuff that would make a videotape of some Muscovite hookers tinkling on a mattress while he and Melania watched seem quaint.

But there's a lot more ground to cover first.

CHAPTER 3
AS IF IN A LABYRINTH

I sold the Renoir and the TV set.
   Don't want to be around when this gets out.
   —Duran Duran, "The Reflex"

YOU WERE GOING to tell me what could possibly be worse—hypothetically speaking—than the rapes, the history of sexual assault, the Putin puppetry, the mob ties, the felony conviction, and Donald Trump's long relationship with the world's most notorious child sex traffickers.

I was, and I will. But we have a lot more to cover before we get there. More than I thought.

Dude, we're 60 pages into this. Are you just jerking me around? Is this going to be like Geraldo Rivera opening Al Capone's vault?

No.

For one thing, Al Capone's vault did not contain a creepy dental chair with weird rubber masks adorning sterile walls:

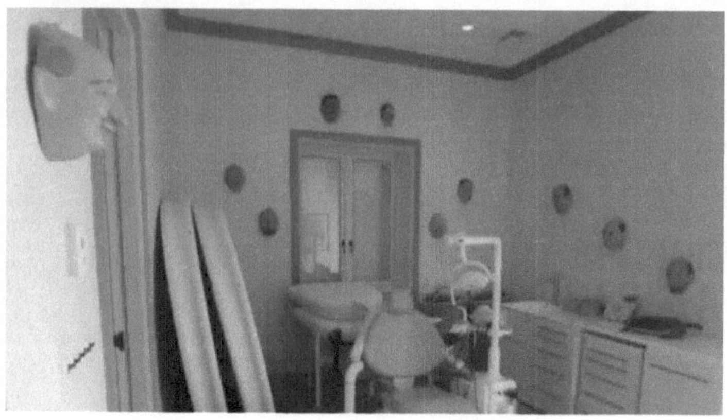

For another, the FBI did not pay a thousand agents a million dollars in overtime to remove stuff from the vault before Geraldo could open it.[1]

Geraldo blocked me on Twitter, by the way. One of my better celebrity blocks.

Why did Geraldo Rivera block you?

I don't remember. Probably I called him a traitor—he was fluffing Trump pretty hard, back in the first term—and clowned him about the empty vault.

I've since reconsidered. What we don't give Rivera enough credit for is, before the unfortunate and embarrassing anticlimax, he managed to get millions of people to watch a long exposé on Al Capone's arrest. That was probably the first time most Americans became aware of money laundering. So maybe I was being a bit too harsh about the empty vault business. Although he totally deserved to be called out for whatever stupid thing he said about Trump.

Very well. The House Oversight Committee released a tranche of photos collected from the Epstein estate.

Indeed.

What's your take on the tranche?

More than half the photos are weird shots of, like, Epstein's hot water heater and the framework on a patio on his island. Not sure why we need to see that.

There are a few photos of Trump with young women and girls—including a blonde in a shoulder-padded blazer whose identity is concealed.

Bill Clinton is there, because there is a little-known Newtonian law of motion that states that for every mention of Trump there must be an equal and opposite mention of Bill Clinton.

There's a funny picture of the credibly accused pedophile formerly known as Prince Andrew, looking like he just sniffed a fart, standing next to Bill Gates. There's also a bunch of shots of Epstein with the leprous Steve Bannon.

But I'm more interested in the other people in the photos.

How so?

I wonder why the Oversight Committee chose to release the material it did. For example, why so many of Woody Allen? Those are relatively recent shots—Allen is there with Bannon, which means it was probably around 2016 or 2017. Noam Chomsky, a known Epstein associate, is in another photo, making Bannon laugh.

Not Chomsky!

Alas, yes. His association with the odious Epstein gives new, and disturbing, meaning to the title of his famous book, *Manufacturing Consent*.

And there are images of people I didn't immediately

recognize. One photo shows Allen, Larry Summers, and his wife, Elisa New, on a private jet; New's "Poetry in America" show was scuttled by PBS almost immediately after the photo was released. (Well done, PBS!)[2]

In another, a grinning Epstein is walking behind the Segway inventor Dean Kamen and Virgin Airlines rich guy Richard Branson, who proudly displays a spiral notebook page. I enhanced the image, like in *Blade Runner*—it's large numbers and the words "million dollars" written in cursive:

Kamen subsequently issued a statement: "I have been a

guest of Richard Branson on his Necker Island a number of times for conferences and fundraisers. I believe this photo must have been taken during one of those events many years ago. I have no knowledge of any of the horrific actions of Jeffrey Epstein other than what I have learned from news reports." Okay, fine, but—if he's not otherwise involved, why show this picture at all?

My favorite image, from a Victoria's Secret public event, shows a submissive-looking Trump trailing behind Epstein, while the Belgian model Ingrid Seynhaeve laughs. I like to think she's laughing *at* Donald.

How is any of that interesting?

I just wonder if there's some larger strategy at work here —if these are "shots across the bow," intended to get people to talk.

For example: In one of the photos, a blonde woman, whose face is obscured, sits at a table—draped, incidentally, with one of the most hideous tablecloths I've ever seen— between Jeffrey and Woody. Who is she? Is she a victim? Is this a ploy to get her to cooperate? Or has she *already* cooperated, and that's why she's redacted—so the others *know* she's cooperating?

Is this 3D chess? Or just random?

Why do you think so many intelligent people stayed close to Epstein, well after the truth came out?

Intelligent people or intelligence people?

Both, I guess?

I'm just kidding. I think.

No, it's true. In the pictures in that tranche alone, we see Gates, Kamen, Chomsky, Woody Allen, Alan Dershowitz, Summers, New, Bill Clinton—a lot of brain power there.

Don't forget about Elon Musk and Peter Thiel. They were both meeting with Epstein, too.

You said intelligent people.

. . .

Ha!

But seriously, it's a good question. Epstein knew any number of academics, scientists, tinkerers, tech pioneers, and so on. Why on earth did these presumptive geniuses stick around?

Philip Weiss probed this question in a 2007 piece for *New York Magazine*.[3] This excerpt is one possible answer to the query:

> "His mind goes through a cross section of descriptions," says Joe Pagano, a financier. "He can go from mathematics to psychology to biology. He takes the smallest amount of information and gets the correct answer in the shortest period of time. That's my definition of IQ."
>
> A Columbia University geneticist says Epstein has that insight in science, too. "He has the ability to make connections that other minds can't make," says Richard Axel, a Nobel Prize winner. "He is extremely smart and probing. He can very quickly acquire information to think about a problem and also to identify biological problems without having all the data that a scientist would have … He also has an extremely short attention span. Why?—it's not that he's bored. He has enough information after fifteen minutes so that you can see his mind thrashing about, as if in a labyrinth. And even to doubt an expert's statements."

What is the sound of one mind thrashing?

No doubt Epstein was smart enough to talk to them on something approaching their level. Which, if you're one of these brainiacs, is probably a welcome development.

These were scientists and researchers from, like, MIT and Harvard. I'm sure there were plenty of other people even

**smarter than Jeffrey Epstein who could talk on their level—
or even above it.**

True, true. There's more to it than that. And as you might imagine, it all comes down to money.

As Weiss also points out, "Epstein has been a munificent supporter of cutting-edge research."

You don't bite the hand that feeds you—even if that hand looks like this:

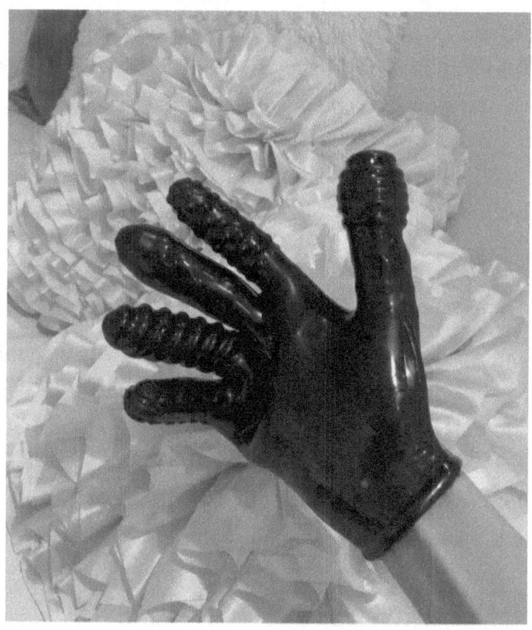

Dude, I just ate breakfast.

Sorry.

And then there's the girls. However brilliant these men might have been, they're also...how shall I put this?...let's just say that on the Venn diagram of human social groups, there is significant overlap between the cohort of tech and science guys Epstein courted and the incel community. In what other reality is, say, Marvin Minsky going to have a young woman who looks like a runway model fawn over him?

I don't necessarily trust the columnist Michael Wolff, but I'm sure the quote from him in Weiss's piece is an accurate summation of how a charming sex trafficker wooed smart, sexually frustrated men:[4]

> *Vanity Fair* columnist Michael Wolff met him in the Internet bubble, in the late nineties, when Epstein invited him and a group of scientists and media types to fly to a conference on the West Coast in his beautiful 727.
>
> "It was all a little giddy," Wolff says. "There's a little food out, lovely hors d'oeuvre. And then after fifteen to twenty minutes, Jeffrey arrives. This guy comes onboard: He was my age, late forties, and he had a kind of Ralph Lauren look to him, a good-looking Jewish guy in casual attire. Jeans, no socks, loafers, a button-down shirt, shirttails out. And he was followed onto the plane by—how shall I say this?—by three teenage girls not his daughters. Not adolescent girls. These are young, 18, 19, 20, who knows? They were model-like. They towered over Jeffrey. And they immediately began serving things. You didn't know what to make of this … Who is this man with this very large airplane and these very tall girls?"

For a lot of those dorks, that's, like, a sexual fantasy come to life.

You said last time that Epstein had Eastern European girls "in his orbit." Who were they?

One of them was Nadia Marcinkova. She was a model from Slovakia. Epstein reportedly referred to her as his "sex slave." He is alleged to have said that he "bought" her from her parents in "Yugoslavia" when she was still a teenager—a claim he later denied making. (Slovakia was never part of Yugoslavia, although there is a country whose name *sounds* like "Slovakia," and that *was* part of Yugoslavia, and whose most famous countryman—Luka Dončić excepted—*is* a key figure in the Russian novel that is the Epstein story; maybe he got them mixed up?)[5]

Tara Palmieri wrote a fantastic piece for POLITICO five years ago that details the many women who worked for Epstein. Of Epstein's Slovakian "assistant," she writes,[6]

> Police reports have stated that another "assistant" of Epstein's, Marcinkova, now 36, engaged in sex acts with Epstein's victims nearly two decades ago. After Epstein was jailed in Florida, she visited him at least 54 times, according to media reports. In a statement to POLITICO, her lawyer said that Marcinkova, too, was victimized by Epstein. According to a Palm Beach police report, Epstein once told a victim that he had purchased Marcinkova at age 15 from her family in Yugoslavia to be his sex slave. "Nadia wants to speak out about her victimization and help Epstein's other survivors," the lawyer's statement said. "Unfortunately, she is not yet able to comment publicly." The lawyer would not say whether Marcinkova has applied for victims' compensation.

Marcinkova, who has a pilot's license—Virginia Heffernan wrote a nice piece about the "Global Girl" right after Epstein croaked[7]—had been holed up in an apartment on the Upper East Side but fled New York right around the time the first batch of Epstein files were released in January 2024.[8] There was some concern that she'd followed Jeffrey to the sweet hereafter, but the intrepid reporter Amber Woods tracked her down to an undisclosed *White Lotus* Season Three-style Buddhist retreat.[9]

Another "assistant," Adriana Ross, née Mucinska, came to Florida from Poland when she was 19, where she hooked up with Epstein in Palm Beach. Holly Baltz of the *Palm Beach Post* notes that Ross[10]

> has been the most silent among Epstein's 'potential co-conspirators' named in his 2007 non-prosecution agreement....
>
> Asked during civil litigation about Prince Andrew and Bill Clinton, Ross, now 41, repeatedly invoked her Fifth Amendment right against self-incrimination. She flew alongside Clinton in Epstein's jet.
>
> She is reportedly living in Miami.

Wait—aren't those two of the four "unindicted co-conspirators" named in Epstein's 2008 non-prosecution agreement?[11]

Correct. Sarah Keller and Leslie Groff, both American-born, are the other two.

Wasn't there a Russian woman who did PR work for Epstein?

That would be Masha Bucher, née Mariia Drokova, usually known in the press as Masha Drokova. And there's a *lot* of press about her: *Byline Times*, *TechCrunch*, *Kyiv Insider*, *WaPo*. Which makes sense, because her job was literally to get press.

Bucher rose to prominence in her native country as the face of Nashi, a pro-Putin youth group—there's a documentary about her, even, called *Putin's Kiss*—but subsequently repudiated Putin, publicly, while still in Russia, after learning about how he treats dissident journalists. She came to the United States on an "Einstein" visa, with referrals from former U.S. ambassador to Russia Michael McFaul and tech analyst extraordinaire Esther Dyson. Per *Wapo*:[12]

> McFaul said while he hadn't followed her career in the United States, her "defection from Nashi, which was when I was serving in Moscow, generated attention—good attention in my view—about the Kremlin's role in sponsoring Nashi."
>
> "I liked her and thought she deserved a chance to live in the U.S.," Dyson told The Post.

Once here, Bucher set up a PR company, leveraged every contact she could find—including the Russian investor and Singapore resident Serg Bell, whom she (supposedly) met on Twitter—and moved from that to venture capital.

And yes, for a year or so, she did PR work for Epstein.

Why would *she* get an Einstein visa? Aren't those for extraordinary ability?

Go read those articles about her, and then come back here and tell me again that she doesn't have extraordinary ability.

A Putin Youth girl turned anti-Putin California-based entrepreneur? With ties to questionable Russian capital? Come on, dude. That's straight out of *The Americans*.

Is it?

I think it's really hard for us soft, pampered Americans to appreciate how lousy it was to grow up in a Communist country in the 80s—or Russia under Vladimir the Puny in the 2000s. The contrast between, say, Prešov, ČSSR, and New York, New York is profound—even if you come from a family of some means, as Nadia Marcinkova did (her father is a prominent architect).

And not every person born in Russia is a Kremlin operative. In the case of Drokova/Bucher, I mean, what else was she supposed to do? She was in Nashi as a teenager, but so what? We happily embrace MAGA youth who see the light—we're in the process of welcoming *Marjorie Taylor Greene* into polite society, ffs; how is that any different?

Bucher stood up to Putin while still in Russia. She networked like crazy. She navigated the move to the U.S.—and the fraught situation with Russian capital after the invasion of Ukraine—and now has a successful investment business. She's done really well for herself.

But Masha worked for Epstein!

Yeah, for a year and half. When she first got here. Before she knew any better. Because that's where her networks led her.

And then, once she realized the deal, *she distanced herself from him*. Which is more than I can say about Bill Gates, Larry Summers, Woody Allen, Peter Thiel, Noam Chomsky, Jes Staley, and the list goes on. And those are men of means, with actual power.

I just think there's a lot of hypocrisy regarding who we condemn and who we let off the hook. So I'm giving Masha Bucher the benefit of the doubt.

Her sister, Victoria, was also in Epstein's orbit.

Yes, she was. She was business partners with Svetlana Pozhidaeva. But mostly she works for oligarchs, as *Byline Times* reports:[13]

Much of Victoria's business career consists of work for entities closely connected to Russian oligarchs and former Chelsea owner Roman Abramovich. According to her Facebook account, she previously worked for a Russian investment advisory firm named Invest AG, which manages the money of Alexander Abramov and Alexander Frolov. Those two own Russia's largest steel company Evraz, and have been known to be close associates of Abramovich. Both were sanctioned by the UK in November 2022.

Financial activity was substantial. Leaked Russian banking records show nearly $60 million moved through three brokerage accounts held by Victoria in 2020-2021. Russian property files list her residence in an elite Moscow complex valued at $1 million.

The thing is, half of London worked for Abramovich at one point, including every player on Chelsea, the football team he owned.

Who is Svetlana "Lana" Pozhidaeva?

Epstein's more recent "assistant." The Dossier Center explains her significance:[14]

Pozhidaeva is a Russian national, who has a long history of business relations with Epstein. According to her, after graduating from the Moscow State Institute of International Relations (MGIMO) she was working as a financial analyst when she made it to the final round of a beauty contest run by the Maxim men's magazine, signed a contract with the Elite Models modeling agency and moved to Europe. How exactly she met Epstein is unknown—a *Daily Mail* source claimed that the billionaire offered her an opportunity to study and "attend conferences with academics." In December 2010, she was photographed for the first time leaving Epstein's mansion while Prince Andrew, the British prince later accused of sexual assault, was staying there. Pozhidaeva denied that she was the woman in the photograph, although, as the *Daily Mail* pointed out, the woman's bag had a Russian airline Aeroflot tag with her name on it. Pozhidaeva then became President of the Education Advance organization, with some of the donations made by Epstein. In a conversation with *The Daily Beast*, Pozhidaeva's boyfriend claimed she knew almost nothing about Epstein's criminal activities and promised to return Epstein's donation.

In 2018, Svetlana launched the WE Talks: the Women's Empowerment project to support female entrepreneurs. Epstein's lawyer Darren Indyke filed the paperwork to register the WE Talks trademark, and the address entered on the application form was the same as that of the Epstein Foundation. After the billionaire's death, Pozhidaeva changed her lawyer.

Darren Indyke. That name comes up a lot in those Epstein emails.

Eleven thousand eighteen times, according to a database search I just did. Atticus Johnson of the *Cornell Daily Sun*, the student paper at Indyke's alma mater, explains that the attorney[15]

worked in Palm Beach as Epstein's personal lawyer, representing him in court in the U.S. Virgin Islands. He was **sued** along with Richard Kahn, Epstein's accountant, in 2024, by two of Epstein's victims for sending payments from Epstein's accounts to victims and knowingly benefitting from participating in Epstein's sex crimes, among six other charges, but he **denied wrongdoing** in the case.

The case is still **ongoing**.

The Cornell Law grad, who has been **described** as a "staple of every [Epstein] event" by a lawyer for Epstein's victims, handled press inquiries for Epstein and frequently forwarded him news articles regarding legal cases against him, according to the released emails. Indyke now works for **Parlatore Law**, a D.C.-based firm with **strong ties** to Trump and represents current U.S. Secretary of Defense Pete Hegseth.

Yikes.

Another Epstein lawyer, Reid Weingarten, also went to law school in Ithaca. The *Daily Sun* explains:[16]

Weingarten, an anti-corruption prosecutor **turned** white collar defense attorney, maintained close ties with Epstein. He was mentioned 109 times in the trove of released emails, where his correspondences reveal a decade-long personal relationship with Epstein beyond legal representation.... After Trump was elected president, the two traded thoughts about politics until Epstein's death.

Almost as embarrassing for Cornell as Leonard Leo being an alumnus.

Half the emails involve Epstein talking to lawyers, it seems like.

Well, I mean, he was a fucking criminal, so it tracks. But yes. Indyke, Weingarten, Alan Dershowitz, Kathryn Ruemmler—attorneys all.

. . .

I know that Epstein was their client. But still. Is it just me, or is it icky?

It's a bedrock principle of the American legal system that everyone is entitled to legal representation. As we all know from Hollywood, the state even *provides* an attorney, if someone under arrest cannot afford one.

But *those* attorneys knew damn well what Jeffrey Epstein was. *They* knew more than *anyone*. Because he could tell them whatever he wanted, and they couldn't say shit. It's all attorney-client-privileged information. That's why the press doesn't press them.

With that said, this isn't Soviet Russia. Indyke and Weingarten were under no obligation to represent Jeffrey Epstein. They *chose* to do so. And not only to work for him, but extend the relationship into what, from the emails, seems to have transcended the attorney-client dynamic. They were *friends*—or so it appears.

In the case of Weingarten, as the emails show, Epstein wasn't even paying his firm's legal bills—so he had a ready-made excuse to ghost the sex-trafficking scumbag. But Weingarten stuck around until the bitter end.

"Icky" is the most generous adjective I can think of to describe them.

Why did so many women stand by Epstein?

If you think of Epstein as a cult leader, it's a little easier to understand. Men like that prey on troubled women and girls, weaponizing their trauma against them. They know how to fuck with their brains so much that they don't want to leave.

Plus, Epstein was a collector. He collected people. Once you were in his orbit, you tended to remain. He seemed to make a distinction between his victims, the girls he and Ghislaine viewed as disposable, and adult women like the attorney Kathryn Ruemmler. He was generally on good terms with his ex-girlfriends, most notably GMax and Eva Andersson-Dubin.

Finally, we have to bear in mind that, as we've seen with Indyke and Weingarten, it wasn't just the women who stood by him.

The men did, too.

By and large, yes. *Including* Donald Trump. Trump and Epstein were in communication well after their little spat about the Florida property that even Epstein said was a way for Russia to shovel money to Trump.

The emails suggest that the two of them stayed in touch pretty much up until the point where Trump became president, and then things cooled. Epstein appeared to have exquisite intelligence on the inner workings of the Trump White House—even after Bannon's West Wing departure.

But Trump and Epstein *did* have a falling out.

It seemed like Epstein had been promised something—a Cabinet position, perhaps, although the idea that Epstein would sit for questions at a Senate confirmation hearing is far-fetched—only to have Trump dick him over somehow.

My *Five 8* co-host Stephanie Koff suggested that the Bannon-Epstein bromance was borne of a mutual anti-Trump grievance. A sort of "the enemy of my enemy is my friend" kind of deal.

Is there any legitimacy to the new $310 million lawsuit accusing Trump, Bill Gates, and Elon Musk of running an "Epstein-identical trafficking and exploitation venture?"

The complaint was filed in Palm Beach County, Florida, on November 24, 2025.[17] There are two plaintiffs. One is a minor.

The other is a woman who claims to be the inventor of "SAFE cybersecurity platform and Abrahamic Accords defense architecture" and also *[checks notes]* some sort of prophylactic gel?

I found this hard to wrap my head around even *before* the sudden modulation into first person at the sixth bullet point:

- Defendant Elon Musk, acting in concert with the Trump administration via the Department of Government Efficiency (DOGE), has used Plaintiff's SAFE cybersecurity platform and Abrahamic Accords defense architecture to secure Elon Musk over $580 billion in federal contracts while refusing to compensate Plaintiff or procure her technology via mandatory sole-source FAR provisions.
- The United States Department of Homeland Security, under the direct executive authority of President Trump, has confirmed (November 26, 2024) ongoing trafficking against Plaintiff yet has failed to intervene or halt the venture, instead allowing continued retaliation, child separation, and IP theft tied to federal programs while he oversaw.
- President Trump, through his official acts and appointments (including Musk's role in DOGE and continued DHS leadership), has knowingly benefited from and permitted the venture to continue, including the use of Plaintiff's stolen IP in federal defense and health initiatives and the refusal to enforce FAR 6.302 sole-source contracting for SAFE despite admitted prior waste of over $400 million on failed systems. He has been supporting foreign attacks instead of American defense from Hamas, Russia, China, and India through Stargate,

the suppression of the FBI, and the suppression
of DHS.

- Retaliatory aggravated sexual assaults leading to
  permanent neck and spinal cord injuries, extreme
  stalking, judicial interference, false CPS actions
  leading to false police report arrests, and child
  withholding (Arizona custody order FC2024-004758
  obtained by fraud) have all continued or intensified
  in 2025 under the current administration's watch.
- Trump bypassed Congress to send over $30 billion
  in direct military aid to Israel through suppressing
  their defense of Israel in 2025 while simultaneously
  endorsing the "Gaza takeover" plan. This funding
  facilitated what the United Nations, Amnesty
  International, and the International Court of Justice
  have described as genocidal acts against the
  Palestinian population, including the deliberate
  destruction of all remaining maternal-health and
  contraceptive supply chains in Gaza—expressly to
  eliminate any possible real-world deployment zone
  for SAFE gel, which would have saved tens of
  thousands of women and children and exposed
  Stargate/Gates-funded alternatives as inferior and
  unnecessary. The Gates Foundation's simultaneous
  $2.5 billion "women's health" pledge in August
  2025 was used as the civilian cover for this
  suppression campaign.
- Terrorism for fear installation including facilitating
  the Baltimore Bridge attack on the day my daughter
  was born March 26th using my ex James Cook, a
  violent rape right before she was born to sabotage
  the birth as well, and then a russian cyberattack on
  the airports using my competitors at Microsoft
  through the Crowdstrike attack, while taking my
  home from me in DC and trying to force me to fly

home to Nebraska during that time where he shortly after had me arrested to prevent me from filing any police reports as confirmed by arresting police investigators of his actors.

- Defendants and their agents have attempted to murdered ###### no fewer than five (5) separate occasions between 2023 and November 2025, including but not limited to poisoning, vehicular assaults, and orchestrated physical attacks designed to appear accidental. Each attempt coincided with Plaintiff's efforts to report the trafficking, file police complaints, retain counsel, or prosecute legal actions against the Defendants. Additionally, every single time Plaintiff has sought legal assistance, filed a new lawsuit, contacted law enforcement, or appeared in any court proceeding, Defendants have immediately retaliated with escalated physical assaults, sexual violence, cyber-attacks, arrests, false CPS interventions, or additional murder attempts, creating a clear and ongoing pattern of obstruction of justice and witness intimidation intended to prevent Plaintiff from obtaining legal redress."

I have not read the whole thing carefully, but I did not find a reference to an attorney for the plaintiff in the complaint, the story at Boca News Now, or anywhere else. If there's no attorney, that suggests that not a single lawyer in Florida, even the ambulance-chasing Saul Goodmans on the billboards, thought the plaintiffs had a snowball's chance of even *settling* with two of the wealthiest men in the world, let alone winning a judgment.

Let's just say that if the plaintiff winds up being awarded $310 million, I will be very surprised.

· · ·

How was Epstein connected to the Kremlin?

He'd been liaising on some level with the Russian intelligence services since his arms-dealer days with Douglas Leese. Perhaps his closest Kremlin contact was Vitaly Churkin, the child actor turned diplomat. There's numerous references to Churkin in the Epstein emails—and he seemed to be scurrying around to find a new Kremlin intermediary to replace Churkin after his death in 2017.

As the indispensable Dave Troy points out at *America 2.0*, Churkin helped plan and manage Trump's first visit to Moscow in 1987. So all of these people have known each other for decades:[18]

> From a historical perspective, it would be difficult to find four people closer to the Russian worldview and the KGB's long-term projects than [former KGB head] Kryuchkov, [legendary KGB operative] Borovik, Churkin, and Trump—and that's exactly the circle in which Epstein was operating. Churkin, who first met Trump in 1986, died February 20, 2017, reportedly from a heart attack—just a day before his sixty-fifth birthday.

Was Epstein ever in Russia?

We know Epstein visited Россия at least once. In April 1998. With the aforementioned tech journalist and Internet champion Esther Dyson—whose influential book, *Release 2.0: A Design for Living in the Digital Age,* had come out the year before. He was photographed in front of the home of the late Andrei Sakharov, the physicist and Nobel Peace Prize laureate, in the closed city of Arzamas-16 (now Sarov).

The photo is still up on her Flickr page, with this caption: "Esther, Jeffery Epstein, Pavel Oleynikov. Sarov is a (former) Soviet 'closed city' where they developed bombs."[19]

As Dave Troy reports at *America 2.0*:

Dyson, who has had a decades-long association with Russia, resigned from the board of Yandex, a Russian search engine company, in protest of Putin's 2022 invasion of Ukraine. She had this to say about her own passing association with Epstein:

...I did meet Epstein myself in Russia courtesy of Nathan Myhrvold, whom I was traveling with around Russia in 1998, to "save Soviet science." Nathan said a Wall Street/finance friend of his would be passing through Sarov at the same time as us, and there's a Flickr photo taken by a friend, of Epstein and me in front of Sakharov's house. ... Also, I met him again later through John Brockman, who was both my father's and my brother's agent.

Dyson asserted that she was not traveling *with* Epstein that day her widely-shared photo in front of Sakharov's house was taken, but that he had essentially dropped in unannounced on Myhrvold when Dyson happened to be present. Myhrvold (who had been suggested by Epstein to Sergei Belyakov as a potential participant in the St. Petersburg International Economic Forum), was at the time a prominent Microsoft executive and interested in the state of Soviet science, as was Epstein—like Robert Maxwell before him.

During the late 90s, Epstein was actively working to penetrate Silicon Valley, and established many contacts there, especially at Microsoft—hence his bromance with Nathan Myhrvold.

Why does that name sound familiar?

From the "birthday book." Myhrvold was the "friend" who sent photographs of wild animals getting busy. He is listed, by the way, in the "friends" section and not the "science" section of that book.

. . .

Gross. And Sergei Belyakov?

The crack investigative team at the Dossier Center[20]

uncovered [Jeffrey Epstein's] close contacts with Sergei Belyakov, then Deputy Minister of Economic Development and later head of the St. Petersburg Economic Forum Foundation, which runs the St Petersburg International Economic Forum (SPIEF). It has become the norm for female escorts from all over Russia to be present at the Forum.

Belyakov is a graduate of the FSB Academy which prepares Russian intelligence officers. As the Dossier Center discovered, he helped Epstein to deal with a Russian model who was blackmailing American businessmen, as well as proposing to arrange meetings with Deputy Finance Minister Sergei Storchak and Central Bank Deputy Chairman Alexei Simanovsky. For his part, Epstein advised Belyakov on saving the Russian economy amid imposed sanctions, while also recruiting high-profile guests for SPIEF.

Basically, Epstein was treasoning with this guy.

Who is John Brockman?

A big-wheel literary agent for, basically, the type of scientists and other big brains whose friendship Epstein was cultivating.

As an author and an editor, Brockman has produced such notable books as *Digerati: Encounters with the Cyber Elite; My Einstein: Essays by Twenty-four of the World's Leading Thinkers on the Man, His Work, and His Legacy; The Third Culture: Beyond the Scientific Revolution;* and *We Are So Much Smarter Than You, You Drooling Peasant.* (I'm pretty sure I made the last one up.) He also headed up The Edge Foundation—"The Edge" as in "the cutting edge," not the guitarist for U2—and hosted "billionaire dinners," where his clients hobnobbed with the über wealthy.

Evgeny Morozov over at the *New Republic,* himself a client of the literary agency, reports that Brockman is "no mere literary agent; he is a true 'organic intellectual' of the digital revolution, shaping trends rather than responding to them." In his TNR piece—titled "Jeffrey Epstein's Intellectual Enabler"—Morozov explains:[21]

> Epstein participated in the Edge Foundation's annual questions, and attended its "billionaires' dinners." Brockman may also be the reason why so many prominent academics—from Steven Pinker to Daniel Dennett—have found themselves answering awkward questions about their associations with Epstein; they are clients of Brockman's. Marvin Minsky, the prominent MIT scientist who surfaced as one of Epstein's island buddies? A client of Brockman's. Joi Ito, the director of the elite research facility MIT Media Lab, who has recently acknowledged extensive ties to Epstein? Also, a client of Brockman's.

Brockman tried, it appears, to lure Morozov into the Epstein spider's web. In the article, Morozov reproduces an entire email Brockman sent him—in 2013, long after the truth about Jeffrey was well known to anyone curious enough to find out. It's a remarkable piece of correspondence from an American agent to his Belarusian client:[22]

> *Jeffrey Epstein, the billionaire science philanthropist showed up at this weekend's event by helicopter (with his beautiful young assistant from Belarus). He'll be in Cambridge in a couple of weeks asked me who he should meet. You are one of the people I suggested and I told him I would send some links.*
>
> *He's the guy who gave Harvard [$]30m to set up Martin Nowak. He's been extremely generous in funding projects of many of our friends and clients. He also got into trouble and spent a year in jail in Florida.*
>
> *If he contacts you it's probably worth your time to meet him as he's extremely bright and interesting.*

Last time I visited his house (the largest private residence in NYC), I walked in to find him in a sweatsuit and a British guy in a suit with suspenders, getting foot massages from two young well-dressed Russian women. After grilling me for a while about cyber-security, the Brit, named Andy, was commenting on the Swedish authorities and the charges against Julian Assange.

"We think they're liberal in Sweden, but its more like Northern England as opposed to Southern Europe," he said. "In Monaco, Albert works 12 hours a day but at 9pm, when he goes out, he does whatever he wants, and nobody cares. But, if I do it, I'm in big trouble." At that point I realized that the recipient of Irina's foot massage was his Royal Highness, Prince Andrew, the Duke of York.

Indeed, a week later, on a slow news day, the cover of the NYpost had a full-page photo of Jeffrey and Andrew walking in Central Park under the headline: "The Prince and the Perv." (That was the end of Andrew's role at the UK trade ambassador.)

Wow. That has the tone of a high school freshman who desperately wants the upperclassmen to think he's cool because he goes to parties on the local college campus.

Or the other way around—an old guy past his prime trying to impress the kids.

But Morozov isn't done with him. Behold the kill shot:[23]

A close analysis of Edge Foundation's (publicly available) financial statements suggests that, between 2001 and 2015, it has received $638,000 from Epstein's various foundations. In many of those years, Epstein was Edge's sole donor. Yet, how many of Edge's contributors—let alone readers—knew Epstein played so large a role in the organization?

So: yeah. Intellectual enabler.

In *The Third Culture*, Brockman writes, "Throughout history, only a small number of people have done the serious thinking for everybody," which I guess explains why none of these eggheads *seriously thought* that Jeffrey Epstein was a bad dude.

Did Epstein in any way facilitate Russian interference in the 2016 election?

It's certainly possible, although that remains to be seen. Epstein was reportedly in possession of kompromat on Trump. Putin is reportedly in possession of kompromat on Trump. Maybe they were in a support group?

But seriously—remember that at the time of his 2016 election victory, Donald was in debt to the tune of $300 million.[24] His son-in-law and shadow president, Jared Kushner, was also in dire financial straits because of his idiotic decision to overpay for 666 Fifth Avenue five minutes before the real estate market collapsed. Handing the nuclear codes to two near bankrupts, needless to say, was ill-advised.

Epstein was likely in a position to know about—if not help facilitate—whatever underhanded financial hijinks Trump was up to at that time.

Was Epstein working for the Russians?

Jeffrey Epstein worked *with* the Russians, for sure. He wasn't working *for* them. He also worked *with* the Israelis—specifically AMAN, the military intelligence unit once headed by his old chum Ehud Barak. But he wasn't working *for* them. Nor was he working *for* MI6, or the Saudis, or the CIA (despite what he was telling women back in the 80s). I don't think he had any allegiance to any one country, intelligence service, or person—other than himself.

Jeffrey Epstein was working for Jeffrey Epstein, just like Robert Maxwell was working for Robert Maxwell.

Here's a question: If Epstein filled the Robert Maxwell void after Robert Maxwell's suspicious death, is there someone filling the Jeffrey Epstein void after Jeffrey Epstein's suspicious death?

"obsessively secretive"

"knows everyone."

"the sort of guy who will turn up behind you on a flight to Rio"

"a real man of mystery"

"unbelievably connected"

"our modern version of a homeless billionaire…constantly working, constantly traveling"

"Rolodex off the charts for someone so young"

"collects people"

"a Zelig-like quality"

Sounds like Epstein, right? But those quotes are from a *Financial Times* article on the press-averse, secrecy-obsessed British billionaire Ian Osborne, 43, whom the *Telegraph* calls the "fixer to the elite"—another descriptor befitting of Epstein.[25]

Ian Osborne? I have never heard of this guy.

Neither had I.

Although their relationship would not be public knowledge until well after the pedophile sex trafficker's 2019 death, Epstein seems to have taken Osborne under his wing back in 2011—at least, that's what we glean from the many hundreds of Ian Osborne-related emails in the Epstein Files.

It may be that, having his aura of invincibility punctured after doing time in prison, Epstein realized the importance of succession planning. Perhaps he saw a little of himself in the young British arriviste.

What did they have in common?

Like Epstein, Osborne is ruthlessly ambitious. Like Epstein, Osborne emerged out of nowhere, with zero practical experience in the field. Like Epstein, he immediately Tom Ripley'd himself into the good graces of a billionaire—Mike Bloomberg, in his case. Like Epstein, he operates in the shadows. Like Epstein, he appears to have a casual relationship with morality. And like Epstein, he knows everyone.

Ian Osborne is everywhere and nowhere all at once.

"It sounds an easy thing to do but connecting people is a rare talent," one rich guy told *FT*. "Dozens of people around the world that Mike [Bloomberg] and I have good relationships with were introduced by Ian. Global business leaders never meet without a go-between. There is no Yellow Pages for that."

There is also no Yellow Pages for the sex trafficking of minors for the purpose of elite sexual exploitation.

Is there a Yellow Pages for *anything* anymore? Does anyone under the age of 40 know what the Yellow Pages even are?

Probably not.

But we should make very clear up front that an important distinction between the dead American "fixer to the elite" and the living British one is that, unlike Epstein, *Ian Osborne is not, has never been, and hopefully will never be involved in the world's largest child sex trafficking operation.*

Indeed, in the interest of objective journalism, we should probably print Osborne's obligatory statement of Epstein contrition, which ran in the *Telegraph* in February 2026:[26] "I wholeheartedly regret that I ever met or had any association whatsoever with Epstein. I never witnessed, nor was aware of, the repellent and illegal behaviour by him. I am forever sorry for all the people who suffered by him. It was a serious error of judgment and one I bitterly regret."

Attend: not just *wholehearted* regret; *bitter* regret.

If Ian is the Second Coming of Jeff, it's because of his behind-the-scenes, off-the-radar networking prowess, as well as his facility with arcane financial chicanery—and nothing more. Again: ***Ian Osborne is not, has never been, and hopefully will never be involved in the world's largest child sex trafficking operation.***

Okay, okay, we get it. So how did they meet?

During his time in New York, Osborne made the acquaintance of "media-industry types" like Andrew Ross Sorkin and, crucially, Michael Wolff.

The File emails show that, at Wolff's urging, Osborne, Wolff and Epstein met on Saturday, May 7, 2011.[27] Osborne's first visit to Epstein's mansion was on Tuesday, June 14, 2011. That was one day after he sent Epstein this email:[28]

Jeffrey,

• In the time since we met last month, I've reflected on the unique challenges and opportunities of your situation, and I am ready to propose what I believe to be the right strategy.

• I shall send the document by email later today but I wanted to let you know I am planning to stop off in New York en route to San Francisco tomorrow AM.

• If you happen to be around, perhaps we can discuss this in person (together with Michael). If not, then we can certainly do so by phone.

Best wishes,

Ian

The document was indeed sent, although the attachment, alas, does not seem to be available in the Files database.

That sounds like a pitch letter, like Osborne was trying to drum up business.

Yes, it appears that he was angling to add Jeffrey Epstein as a PR client.

If the "unique challenges and opportunities of your situation" is a diplomatic way of addressing the sex-trafficked elephant in the room—and I'm not sure how this can be read in any other way—the email to Epstein seems to contradict Osborne's recent statement of wholehearted and bitter regret, in which he claims he "never witnessed, nor was aware of, the repellent and illegal behaviour by him." We can easily swap out "unique challenges and opportunities of your situation" with "your repellent and illegal behaviour" in that email without changing its meaning.

It seems inconceivable that Osborne didn't have *some* inkling of what Epstein was when he pitched him on the "unique challenges" of his "situation." Are we really to believe that, in the days leading up to their first meeting in May 2011, *Michael Wolff*, of all people, one of the most notorious gossips in New York, didn't dish to Osborne, whose writing profile suggests a similar appetite for salacious tittle-tattle, failed to mention Epstein's sick predilections? Or that Osborne, already well established in the halls of power, didn't hear about Jeffrey Epstein and underage girls? Or that this Xennial mover-and-shaker didn't think to Google "Jeffrey Epstein" and see what popped up in his browser?

I knew about Epstein in 2011, ffs. And I was an obscure novelist in the podunk Hudson Valley, not a fancy big-city PR guy with access to all kinds of intel who was hoping to meet with him.

. . .

So Osborne was connected to Epstein.

Does the Pope wear a funny hat?

The Pope wears a Chicago White Sox hat.

It's just an expression.

What did Epstein get from Osborne?

For one thing, Osborne appears to have connected Jeffrey with Peter Thiel—like Reese of Reese's Pieces fame combining chocolate and peanut butter, but for absolute evil.

Peter Thiel?

Capo di tutti capi of the PayPal Mafia, early investor in Facebook and Twitter, co-founder of the omniscient surveillance company Palantir, owner and sole proprietor of fascist couchfucker JD Vance, sweaty *eminence grise* of the Trump Redux, radical Catholic of the Leonard Leo persuasion, immigrant from Germany via South Africa, billionaire whose politics are to the right of Hammurabi, and philosophy major obsessed with the Antichrist—but then, we're all somewhat obsessed with ourselves.

Osborne hooked them up. Take a look:

Ian Osborne <Ian Osborne>   Nov 2, 2011 5:56 AM
to jeevacation@gmail.com, jeevacation@gmail.com

Yes definitely. I will call Peter today w/ background.

Sent from my iPhone

On 1 Nov 2011, at 07:02, Jeffrey Epstein jeevacation@smail.com> wrote:

can you set up a telephone call with peter thiel.?

How can it be that I've never heard of this guy?

Osborne remains an obscure figure in the United States. A gander at a list of my sourcing reveals primarily European publications: the *Guardian*, the *Telegraph*, the *Financial Times*: all British. *Business Insider* is based in New York but is owned by the German media company Axel Springer SE. *Le Monde* ran a piece in February about Epstein's attempts to influence the Sarközy government, in which Osborne is mentioned.[29]

Those are all, notably, foreign sources. In the U.S., Ian Osborne has managed to avoid media scrutiny. He is mentioned fleetingly in a few longer *New York Times* pieces on Epstein. But as best as I can tell, an American legacy media outlet has yet to do a profile on *him*. Even Bloomberg News has been conspicuously silent on the subject of its billionaire founder's former advisor.

What this means is that the American public, which gets the lion's share of its news from American media, has never heard of the guy. Stop a thousand people on the street and ask them who he is, and they'd probably guess he's Ozzy's son.

It's almost like Ian Osborne doesn't exist.

Epstein would approve.

Did they work together on anything?

Yes. The two of them joined forces on a 2012 mission to install their mutual banking buddy Jes Staley as CEO of Barclays.

Staley is the JPMorgan Chase wealth management guy who wrote to Epstein, after Epstein got out of jail: "The strength of a Greek army was that its core held shoulder to shoulder, and would not flee or break, no matter the threat. That is us."

Epstein and Osborne even had a name for the mission. They called it—drumroll, please—"Project Jes."

How creative.

This is from the Kalyeena Makortoff story in the *Guardian*:[30]

> Evidence presented to the upper tribunal in London showed that Epstein began emailing a man named Ian Osborne in summer 2012 with the subject heading "Project Jes", seemingly in an effort to promote Staley's prospects of becoming the chief executive of Barclays. Barclays was searching for a replacement for Bob Diamond, who had been forced out by the Libor fixing scandal.
>
> One of the emails sent by Ian Osborne—who ran a press relations and business development consultancy—to Epstein claimed he had access to the then chancellor, George Osborne, and hoped to influence top-level officials at the Bank of England.
>
> "Let me know how you want to proceed and I will get on it, calls can happen anytime and I can see people back in London after Tuesday," the email said. "Rupert and George are both very close to Mervyn King and top BoE [Bank of England] staff. I am seeing the chancellor anyway next Thursday."
>
> Previous evidence outlined by the FCA showed that Epstein and Ian Osborne also discussed contacting the Barclays deputy chair Mike Rake as part of their efforts. "I won't do anything before hearing back from you but I'm ready to go into bat for our friend," Ian Osborne said.

Are we *sure* Osborne's not a sex trafficker?

Again: he is absolutely not! Please don't get that idea!

Part of me feels a little bad, putting him in this Epstein Q&A. But here's the thing: If Ian Osborne didn't want to be associated with the most notorious child sex trafficker in recent memory, Ian Osborne should not have associated himself with the most notorious child sex trafficker in recent memory.

Also, his company is called Hedosophia, which we're told, in Epstein Files emails, derives from the Greek words for *pleasure* and *knowledge* smashed together. But it's also one letter away from "Pedosophia," which would mean "knowledge of pedophiles."

Was that intentional?

No. But still. If he hired Masha Bucher to do his PR, she'd have come up with a better name.

Ha!

And now, somehow, we're once again over 8,000 words, so we have to wind this chapter up.

CHAPTER 4
TOTALLY TRICKED OUT BY UNCLE JEFFREY TODAY!

See the pyramids along the Nile,
  Watch the sunrise on a tropic isle,
  Just remember, darling, all the while,
  You belong to me.
  —Jo Stafford

———

SO WHAT'S **the deal with Epstein's properties? Isn't there, like, a whole other island next to Little St. James that no one knows about?**

There is: Great St. James. I'd never heard of this island until Amber Woods, an investigative journalist, wrote about it on her Substack:[1]

The island has underwater utilities carved into the coastline, a solar array big enough to power something far larger than a cottage, and a structure described—casually, almost innocently—as a "pool and underwater office."

We don't know the full footprint of that "office" or its use.

But from looking at the (low quality) satellite imagery:

whatever it is, it likely lives beneath that deceptively small "pool" with a thick concrete base. This is likely an entry point to an underground facility of some kind.

The purchase was shrouded in secrecy:

Great St. James was acquired in 2016 through a shell structure designed to conceal true ownership. The community didn't want Epstein (by then, a convicted sex offender) to own it. Residents protested. Local officials hesitated. But the purchase went through anyway. Strangely, under a name that wasn't his. He used the name of an associate and Dubai businessman Sultan Ahmed bin Sulayem.

Weird shit is going on on that island, Woods suggests. Same thing at Zorro Ranch.

Zorro Ranch?

Epstein's property in New Mexico. Also super strange. Woods covers this as well:[2]

The question that sits at the top of every page of this investigation still has no real answer: how did a convicted sex offender obtain a thousands-acre fortress inside one of the most politically connected families' land holdings in New Mexico?

The King family sold him land deep inside their own property.

The State Land Office leased him another thousand acres.

Everyone involved knew who he was. And they gave him a territory so remote and insulated that it virtually erased the outside world.

I will add that the manager at Zorro Ranch, Brice Gordon,

and his wife, Karen, have gone to ground.[3] That happened right after Epstein's death.

I shudder to think what all of this means. But what it suggests, to me, is that whatever diabolical shit Epstein was up to in the Virgin Islands and in the desert continues apace.

What do you make of the Alisa Valdes-Rodriguez story?
Which one? She's on an absolute heater lately.

The one about Zorro Ranch and the comms networks.
Ah, yes. The piece with this oh-so-subtle title:

Ghislaine Maxwell's Father Sold Bugged Israeli Software to Two Nuclear Weapons Labs in New Mexico. Then His Daughter Led Jeffrey Epstein to Purchase a Ranch Located Halfway Between Them.

A federal paper trail connects Robert Maxwell's bugged software at Sandia to Epstein's Zorro Ranch, the Huffines family's secret Moscow meeting, and a son in the Trump White House.

ALISA VALDES-RODRIGUEZ
MAR 26, 2026

Wait—there are *two* nuclear labs in New Mexico?
Right? I didn't know that, either.

Even folks who (wisely) saw *Barbie* instead of *Oppenheimer* know about Los Alamos. The other one, Sandia

National Laboratories, is on an Air Force base in Albuquerque.

A lab in Albuquerque, you say? Are we sure it isn't Walter White and Jesse Pinkman?
No, smart-ass. Although things sure did break bad.
I'll let Valdes-Rodriguez explain:[4]

It is one of three Department of Energy nuclear research facilities, responsible for the non-nuclear components of American nuclear weapons — the triggering systems, the delivery mechanisms, the engineering that makes a warhead function. Los Alamos National Laboratory, roughly ninety miles northwest, is where the weapons themselves are designed, and where J. Robert Oppenheimer's team created the world's first atomic bomb. Together, these two New Mexico facilities represent the operational core of the American nuclear arsenal.

It always seemed weird to me that Epstein had a ranch in the New Mexico desert. The Upper East Side mansion? Yes. The Paris flat? *Absolument.* The Palm Beach residence? Sure. Even the two little Virgin Islands make sense. But New Mexico? Why?

Well, it's because the Zorro Ranch—that's what the Epstein compound is called—is smack-dab in the middle of these two nuclear labs. (It's also not that far from Roswell, but let's not go there.)

That could be a coincidence.
When it comes to Jeff Epstein, there are no coincidences. Check out this précis of Zorro Ranch by Valdes-Rodriguez:[5]

The chronology is as follows: Robert Maxwell, alleged Mossad and multi-agency intelligence asset, penetrated Sandia National Laboratories with surveillance software in 1985. His daughter Ghislaine became Jeffrey Epstein's operational partner in the 1990s, after Robert's mysterious death in 1991. Epstein purchased Zorro Ranch — positioned near the midpoint between Sandia and Los Alamos — from the governor of New Mexico, built a private microwave communications link to Sandia Crest, and operated the ranch as a hub of what federal prosecutors described as an international sex trafficking and blackmail network for nearly three decades. Upon Epstein's death, his estate — including Zorro Ranch — passed to Karyna Shuliak, a Belarusian national introduced to Epstein through Russian contacts, who was in Russia the day he died. The ranch was subsequently sold to a Texas family whose documented Russian contacts include a secret Moscow meeting with sanctioned officials, whose son sits in the Trump White House, and who has kept Epstein's private microwave link to Sandia Crest running in Epstein's company name.

There's basically a closed-circuit communications network running between Zorro Ranch and the Sandia Crest Tower, near the lab:

FCC records show that Zorro Development Corp., registered at 49 Zorro Ranch Road, Stanley, New Mexico, holds two active Microwave Industrial/Business Pool licenses — call signs WQXY316 and WQXY300, both granted July 12, 2016, both expiring July 12, 2026. License WQXY316 carries transmissions from the Zorro Ranch main residence to Sandia Crest Tower in the Sandia Mountains east of Albuquerque. License WQXY300 carries transmissions from Sandia Crest Tower back to Zorro Ranch. Together they constitute a permanent, fixed, bidirectional private microwave communications link — a dedicated two-way data channel operating entirely outside commercial internet infrastructure, through channels where traffic cannot be monitored, intercepted, or logged by third parties.

Microwave...industrial...?

Let Valdes-Rodriguez explain:[6]

To understand the significance of this infrastructure, consider who actually uses Industrial/Business Pool microwave systems: NSA field stations, CIA operational facilities, FBI secure data operations, Department of Defense installations, electric utilities, natural gas pipeline operators, high-frequency trading firms, and major bank data centers. None of those descriptions apply to a private vacation ranch in the high desert.

Okay, that's weird for sure. But Epstein is dead, so what difference does it make?

He's dead—at least, we think he's dead, *pace* all the AI slop of an unkempt Epstein milling around Tel Aviv—but *the calls signs are active.* The LLC is active. It's now owned by Donald Huffines, a Texas MAGA politician and his wife, Mary Catherine Huffines, a ride-or-die Ron Paul disciple who is *so* Russia'd up...

[pauses]

She's *so* Russia'd up...

How Russia'd up is she?

She's *so Russia'd up,* she went with Rand Paul to Moscow

when he hand-delivered the letter from Donald Trump to Vladimir Putin.

Охренеть!

Хорошо сказано.

Wasn't Epstein's last girlfriend Russian? The dentist? Karyna Shuliak?

"Girlfriend" is doing a lot of work in that sentence. She's from Belarus, not Russia.

Valdes-Rodriguez has an interesting theory about her, too. She posits that Shuliak took over Ghislaine Maxwell's role as Epstein's handler after GMax ran afoul of the law. Shuliak, she explains,[7]

came from Belarus — a Russian client state, the last dictatorship in Europe, whose intelligence services are answerable ultimately to Moscow. She spoke fluent English. She was emotionally sophisticated, gracious, already an adult. She was already in her 20s. In college to be a dentist. Confident. With supportive parents.

She was by every account unlike Epstein's type. He preferred desperate children who'd been abused and neglected. Helpless, terrified, tiny people so used to being hurt they did not know how to fight back.

What the DOJ files show about Karyna Shuliak is remarkable for what it excludes. She was verbally and emotionally abusive toward Epstein. She slapped him on multiple occasions. She took control of his household staff, his finances, his schedule. She managed his operations. The terror and degradation that saturates every account of Epstein's actual victims is entirely absent from the accounts involving

Shuliak. She was seemingly never trafficked by him to anyone else.

She appears at the same time Ghislaine is likely headed toward a conviction and jail, too. His former "girlfriend" handler is soon to be incapacitated.

Enter Karyna.

Epstein altered his will two days before he croaked, naming Shuliak as his primary inheritor. After his death, the Zorro Ranch passed to her. She owned it for five years, before selling it to the Huffines.

Guess where she was on the day Epstein died?

Starbucks?

Russia.

That tracks.

Do you think Jeffrey Epstein knew what was coming? That the end was near?

I mean, did Tony Soprano, when he walked into that diner and Journey came on the jukebox?

It's true that Epstein spent the spring of 2019 negotiating the purchase of Bin Ennakhil,[8] an extravagant Moorish palace outside of Marrakesh—in Morocco, a country that, as many commentators have observed, doesn't have an extradition treaty with the United States. That suggests a plan to flee. It's also true that he'd been trying to buy the place for years; from what I gather, the seller was old and eccentric and impossible to deal with.

Did Epstein suspect that the long arm of the law was coming for him when, on March 13, 2019, his request for a multi-million dollar wire transfer was kiboshed by, of all people, Deutsche Bank? How about on June 26th, when he again attempted to wire 11.15 million euros to close the Bin Ennakhil deal? Or on the Fourth of July, when he tried for a third time to transfer the funds? The emails suggest that he and Shuliak planned to visit Marrakesh on July 8.[9]

If that's true, then why did Epstein fly back to the United States from Paris on the 6th? Why didn't he high-tail it to Morocco instead and wait for the money to clear? Are there no good hotels in Marrakesh?

A more pertinent question, perhaps, is: Did *Karyna Shuliak* know what the future held in store for her doomed benefactor?

Fine. Did *Karyna Shuliak* know what the future held in store for her doomed benefactor?

Her activities immediately before and after Epstein's July arrest suggest that she may have had some inkling.

Back in 2013, Shuliak entered into a sham marriage with an ex-girlfriend of Kimbal Musk, Jena Kalin, to facilitate her path to U.S. citizenship. She was granted that citizenship in October of 2018. In November of 2018, just before Julie K. Brown's *Miami Herald* series "Perversion of Justice" dropped, she filed for divorce.

In the winter and spring of 2019, Shuliak was the point person on communications with Marc Leon, the Marrakesh real estate broker; their correspondence went on for weeks.[10] She also made all of the travel arrangements. Her dutiful cancellation of the train tickets from Geneva to Paris (€232 refunded) and Montreax to Geneva (€73.20 refunded), a trip she planned to make on July 8 to collect belongings she'd left in Switzerland, is comical, given the $50 million she stood to inherit five weeks later.

At 8:29 am on Saturday, July 6, Epstein, in one of his last

missives, asked his attorney, Darren Indyke, to "lets =echeck karyna divorce [sic]." Two hours later, Indyke wrote back: "On the docket it looks like it was=granted. I emailed Rachel Ehrlich who should be receiving the judgme=t of divorce (if she hasn't already). I will call her office=on Monday. [sic]."

At 2:49pm, Epstein forwarded that response to Shuliak; he was arrested at Teterboro later that day.

While there are reports of her presence at Teterboro, I can't conclusively determine if Shuliak was with Epstein in New Jersey at the time of his arrest. If so, it looks like she never got off the plane. She was back in Paris on Sunday, July 7th. At least, that's what she told Darren Indyke at 3am that day:[11]

I want to be prepared to go back to NY as soon as I can. I am in Paris now, but need to go back to Montreux, Switzerland to get my belongings (I have been studying at school there for the past 3 weeks, but will have to terminate it for the obvious reason). It is a train ride without passport control. Is it safe if I go there today with and come back to Paris either tonight or tomorrow morning?

Indyke advised her to stay put.

On July 8, the Monday after the Saturday arrest, Shuliak wrote to an interior decorator, who planned to do some work on one of the New York properties on the 9th, "Yes, I am still in Europe. Could you please kindly check with [someone else] if Tuesday is ok."[12]

And then what happened?

After the arrest, her activities get more sus.

On July 30, Shuliak visited Epstein at MCC; from what I can tell, it was the only time she did so.

On August 8, Epstein created a new trust agreement—The 1953 Trust—to her benefit.[13]

Section 2.3. Bequests

A.   I make the following general bequests:

1.   to KARYNA SHULIAK, if she survives me, Fifty Million Dollars ($50,000,000). In addition to said bequest, as soon as practicable after my death, the Trustees are directed to purchase an annuity for the benefit of KARYNA SHULIAK from a reputable financial institution in the amount of Fifty Million Dollars ($50,000,000), which annuity shall be payable monthly for the life of KARYNA SHULIAK. Upon the death of KARYNA SHULIAK, the Trustees shall distribute the remaining principal balance of said annuity, and any income, pro rata to the beneficiaries listed in Article II, Section 2.3(A)(4)-(41) in the same percentage that their initial bequest bears to the total amount of bequests made in Article II, Section 2.3(A)(4)-(41):

It is my intention to fund a separate trust for KARYNA SHULIAK prior to my death. In the event that a separate trust is created and funded by me for KARYNA SHULIAK then the amount bequeathed by this section shall be reduced by the amount of principal conveyed by me to the separate trust.

At 7:19pm on the evening of August 9, 2019, Epstein placed a phone call on "an unsecured and unrecorded line" to Shuliak. They spoke for 19 minutes. Neither the FBI nor the NYPD had any details about the nature of that call.

He was found "unresponsive" at 6:33am the next morning.

"According to information obtained from a BOP Special Investigator Lieutenant and information that was related to her," an email sent on August 11 from someone on the Violent Crimes Task Force reads, "Epstein was found with a torn piece of issued BOP orange colored bedding around his neck with the other end affixed to the bunk bed."[14] That same day, an "autopsy was conducted by the NY Office of the C[h]ief Medical Examiner. The preliminary results indicate the cause of death to be consistent with suicide by hanging."

Where is Karyna Shuliak now?

Dunno. After that, Shuliak vanishes from public view. If the FBI investigated her, there's no record of it I can find.

Even people following the Epstein story know little about Karyna Shuliak. I've been writing about this for years, and she barely registered on my radar. And yet she was in the thick of everything for a full decade.

But we should stick to things we know for sure.

Like what?

Like how a businesswoman named Lynn Forester de Rothschild is who introduced Epstein to Prince Andrew—and how she Forrest Gump'd her way into the same networks Epstein penetrated.

Rothschild Rothschild?

Yes, but no. Her late husband—her third—was Evelyn de Rothschild, of the famous banking family. But she's from New Jersey.

So what's her deal?

Like Epstein, she's a connector. Kaitlyn Pierce—aka Kait Justice—wrote a nice summary of her various Epstein-adjacent associations.[15] As she puts it, "Lynn Forester de Rothschild connects the Clintons, British royalty, the legal protection apparatus, banking infrastructure, and the physical transportation network."

Get a load of *this*:[16]

Her family owned the aviation company at the airport Epstein used more than anywhere else, gave Ghislaine Maxwell housing after Robert Maxwell died, **introduced Epstein to the lawyer who negotiated his plea deal and she joined Deutsche Bank's advisory board** one month before they accepted Epstein as a client despite his conviction. According to Maxwell's own testimony to the Deputy Attorney General, Lynn introduced Epstein to Prince Andrew and there is a letter where she was discussing Epstein with **President Clinton** in 1995.

Pierce offers more detail in her piece about *Eyes Wide Shut*:[17]

[de Rothschild's] documented connections to Epstein's infrastructure include:

Transportation: Her father J. Kenneth Forester founded aviation operations at Teterboro Airport in 1946. Her brother ran Million Air there. Million Air is listed in Epstein's black book.

Housing: According to multiple reports, in 1991, immediately after Robert Maxwell's death, she provided Ghislaine Maxwell a Manhattan apartment. According to Business Insider's review of tax records, in October 2000 she sold a Manhattan townhouse to **a shell company with the same address as Epstein's business office** for approximately $8.5 million below its assessed market value of over $13.4 million. Business Insider noted they could not independently confirm the seller was the same Lynn Forester who appeared in Epstein's flight logs. Maxwell moved into the property.

Banking: According to Der Spiegel, she joined Deutsche Bank's advisory board in July 2013. Consent orders show **Deutsche Bank took on Epstein as a client approximately one month later** despite his registered sex offender status.

Introductions: Alan Dershowitz has publicly stated she introduced him to Epstein, calling him "an interesting autodidact." According to Ghislaine Maxwell's proffer testimony released in 2025, **Lynn Forester de Rothschild introduced Prince Andrew to Epstein.**

Lynn Forester de Rothschild seems important. Why is this the first I've heard of her?

Good question.

. . .

Epstein sure knew a lot of well-connected women.

He did. And they adored him. Peggy Siegel, the Hollywood publicist. The late Clare Hazell-Iveagh—the socialite, interior designer, and wife of Edward "Ned" Guinness, of the famous brewery family, the 4th Earl of Iveagh.

And Kathy Ruemmler, of course.

Kathryn Ruemmler, you mean? President Obama's White House Counsel? The former chief counsel at Goldman Sachs?

That's the one.

Epstein played her like a Stradivarius. Stroked her ego. Played to her vanity. Bought her fancy gifts—clothes and accessories, and also spa trips and that kind of thing. In one email, she writes him, "Am totally tricked out by Uncle Jeffrey today! Jeffrey boots, handbag, and watch!"[18]

Gross. How many Ruemmler emails are there in the Files?

Emails that reference her? Not that many—a mere 7,238.

Kathy Ruemmler	**Re: Jeffrey Epstein** -Kathy! Come at 1pm. See you then! Sent from my iPhone O	**Nov 19, 2014**
Kathy Ruemmler 12	**Re: Jeffrey Epstein** -ok, thanks On Nov 19, 2014, at 1:04 PM, Kathy Ruemmler <	**Nov 19, 2014**
Kathy Ruemmler 6	**(no subject)** -Kathryn Helen **Ruemmler** Passport # ▓▓▓▓ DOB:=19	**Jul 4, 2015**
Kathy Ruemmler	**Re: Jeffrey Epstein** -I am running a few minutes late. Am leaving my office now.	**Nov 19, 2014**
Kathy Ruemmler	**Re: Jeffrey Epstein (again)** -good hands with....! On Apr 4, 2015, at 9:11 PM, Kath	**Apr 5, 2015**
Kathy Ruemmler	**Re: Jeffrey Epstein 2:30pm** -Thank you. See you soon. On Feb 3, 2015 11:10A wr	**Feb 3, 2015**
Kathy Ruemmler	**Re: Jeffrey Epstein** -for the late notice! Kathy > On May 21, 2019, at 2:57 PM, Le	**May 21, 2019**
Kathy Ruemmler	**Re:** -Kathy Ruemmler wrote: You are too generous. Since i am now going to be i	**Dec 26, 2015**
Kathy Ruemmler	**Re: Jeffrey Epstein** -On Apr 22, 2015, at 5:20 PM, Kathy **Ruemmler** wrote: Let's h	**Apr 23, 2015**
Kathy Ruemmler	**Re: Jeffrey Epstein** -Great. 5:15 confirmed Sent from my iPhone On Mar 23, 201	**Mar 23, 2016**

. . .

Seven *thousand*...

...two hundred thirty-eight. And those are just the ones that we have access to. There are others, apparently, that haven't been released because of attorney-client privilege.[19]

Was she his lawyer?

No. Not formally. But she sort of made it seem like she maybe was. In her recent statement about the matter, Ruemmler said, "I was a defense attorney when I dealt with Jeffrey Epstein. I got to know him as a lawyer and that was the foundation of my relationship with him. I had no knowledge of any ongoing criminal conduct on his part, and I did not know him as the monster he has been revealed to be."

Hang on. If Ruemmler was a defense attorney when she dealt with him, and she got to know him as a lawyer, how could she not have been aware of his criminal conduct? Like, why else would a defense attorney get to know him "as a lawyer?"

You tell me, Perry Mason.

Was Ruemmler in contact with Epstein when she was working at the White House?

Yes. For at least a few months. At one point, she allegedly gave him non-public information about an internal White House investigation.

So she *was* a spy?

I wouldn't go that far. The investigation was into a White

House advance staffer, and also some Secret Service guys, getting drunk and soliciting prostitutes during a trip to Cartagena, Colombia.

WaPo did a big story on it in 2014.[20] It was a huge scandal at the time. Imagine! A scandal because a volunteer allegedly hired a prostitute in a city where prostitution is legal! Fast-forward 12 years—one of the world's biggest pimps is the actual president, and half the country doesn't seem to care.

Wait—wasn't Ruemmler floated as an AG candidate when Eric Holder stepped down?

Yes. There are a *lot* of emails in the Files about this. She sent the link to a story about it to Epstein.[21] From what I can tell, they discussed it—but not via email.

But she wasn't nominated.

Ruemmler withdrew her name from consideration.[22] The excuse was that her friendship with Obama would complicate her confirmation. But for all we know, the real reason might have been that she didn't want to have to explain—under oath, before the U.S. Senate—her cozy relationship with a convicted sex offender.

There's a lot to unpack here.

We haven't even scratched the surface.

The relationship was problematic for any number of reasons—not least of which was the fact that, as Kathryn Rubino writes at *Above the Law*, Ruemmler's "literal job description is reputational risk."[23]

Rubino continues:

Ruemmler isn't some inexperienced legal rube who brushed elbows with a toxic client once upon a time. She is the top attorney at Goldman (chief legal officer and general counsel), a member of the management committee, head of the firmwide conduct committee, and co-vice chair of the reputational risk committee. Avoiding the sort of reputational damage that could arise from blurring professional and friendly relations with a toxic client isn't just expected; it's the whole job. Which makes emails calling Epstein "sweetie" while advising him on sexual misconduct allegations feel less like a lapse and more like a flashing red warning light.

Then there are the pricy gifts from Epstein — a $9,400 Hermès bag, a $4,200 Fendi fur-trimmed plaid wool coat, and a $1,700 Fendi bag amongst them. And she dutifully thanked her "Uncle Jeffrey" for the largesse. Now, a spokesperson said, "Ms. Ruemmler didn't ask for anything and didn't want anything," which may well be true, but surely it's obvious that the excessive gifts, and referring to Epstein as family (she also referred to him as an "older brother" in another exchange) is not exactly a master class in character evaluation.

Sounds like she had a blind spot for Epstein.

Totally.

Epstein glamoured her, like Edward from *Twilight*. And Ruemmler was, to paraphrase the British police detective from *The Third Man*, born to be glamoured.

It's astonishing, how far and wide Epstein's network was.

Not was. Is. Present tense. He's gone, but the vacuum has been filled—if not by one individual, then by a few.

• • •

Ian Osborne?

Maybe.

Jared?

There's a dearth of emails in the Files about Jared. So either Epstein kept those discussions offline, or Kushner-related emails are what the DOJ is keeping under wraps. As Nina Burleigh has pointed out, all of Jared's forays into Middle East diplomacy have Epstein's fingerprints all over them.

It's the same cast of characters every time: Israeli intelligence, Russian intelligence, European diplomats, Saudi royals —and, of course, the banks. And one bank in particular.

JP Morgan Chase?

Or "JP Epstein Chase," as I call it.

In the first quarter of 2023, three court cases related to the sex-trafficking operation of the late "financier" and his bank of choice were filed in the Southern District of New York. The three court filings, all contained in one convenient but sometimes confusing PDF, were among the thousands of documents recently released by the Justice Department—part of the so-called "Epstein Files."[24]

On January 10, 2023, the Government of the United States Virgin Islands and the wonderfully-named law firm of Motley Rice sued JP Morgan Chase in a *parens patriae* action—that is, an action on behalf of its citizens—alleging violation of the U.S. Trafficking Victims Protection Act, the Virgin Islands Criminally Influenced and Corrupt Organizations Act, and the Virgin Islands Consumer Fraud and Deceptive Business Practices Act—and seeking damages.

Three days later, the firms of Pottinger Edwards and Boies Schiller Flexner filed a civil class action complaint on behalf of Jane Doe 1 "individually and on behalf of all others similarly situated" against the same JP Morgan Chase, seeking "damages and other relief." The bank, the plaintiffs allege, was liable for "aiding and abetting, intentional infliction of emotional distress, and negligence related to sexual offenses" stemming from its "participation and intentional involvement in Jeffrey Epstein's widespread and well-publicized sex-trafficking operation, as well as the direct financial benefits it received therefrom."

Finally, on March 8, 2013, a third-party complaint was submitted by two rhyming law firms: Massey & Gail and Wilmer Hale. The former was suing JP Morgan Chase on behalf of the USVI; the latter, in the same action, was suing, on behalf of said bank, its erstwhile top executive, James Edward "Jes" Staley. Once the presumptive heir apparent to longtime JP Morgan CEO Jamie Dimon, the disgraced banker stood accused of "indemnity, contribution, breach of fiduciary duty, and breach of the faithless servant doctrine," owing to the untoward nature of his relationship with Jeffrey Epstein.

I don't follow.

In plain English, the Virgin Islands was pointing a finger at JP Morgan, which was pointing a finger at Jes Staley—a sort of jurisprudential state/corporation/human centipede. Taken together, the three lawsuits threatened to cost JP Morgan a pretty penny—and Staley, potentially, even more.

In my reporting on JP Morgan and Jes Staley, I'd come across references to these lawsuits, but I'd never read the full text of any of them before.

And?

It's a lot.

The Jane Doe 1 class action suit is particularly instructive in understanding the role JP Morgan played in both the day-to-day operation and the expansion of the mammoth sex-trafficking enterprise built by Epstein. While it is a subjective document, intended to persuade, there are nevertheless cold hard facts contained therein. Because of discovery, the attorneys had access to internal JP Morgan emails, including exchanges between Staley and Epstein—some innocuous, some enigmatic, some sketchy af.

What matters about the Staley-Epstein relationship is not the bromance itself, but rather that, for many years, including years subsequent to Epstein's initial arrest and non-prosecution agreement, *Staley was acting on behalf of the bank that employed him*. Staley *was* JP Morgan.

At least, that is what the third lawsuit argues. And JP Morgan's attorneys were concerned enough with the allegations to reach settlements, to the tune of $365 million—$75 million to the Virgin Islands[25] and $290 million to Jane Doe 1 and the other survivors.[26]

That sounds like a lot of money, but the bank had a net income of *$14 billion* in the fourth quarter of 2025 alone. Barron's notes that "JPMorgan's stock rose 34% in 2025, and its market value surpassed $900 billion for the first time this month."[27] The good times are rolling!

A million dollars a day for a full year? That's winning the lottery for you and me; for JP Morgan, it's just the cost of doing business.

[long pause]

What is it? Why are you staring off into space like that?

Something just occurred to me.

Epstein was connected to all these intelligence agencies:

U.S., British, Israeli, Russian, Saudi, and then big *machers* from the other Gulf States—the UAE, Qatar, and so on.

But something is missing.

ایران؟

Good catch. If you search the emails for "Iran," and scroll through, it's clear that Epstein didn't seem to care for the Iranians. Nor did any of his associates.

Maybe he developed a distaste for the Revolutionary Guard during his Iran-Contra days?

Could be. Manucher Ghorbanifar, the arms dealer who was the driving force behind that arrangement, was from Iran. Or maybe he got into a disagreement over the embassy he was renting from the Iranians before he moved to Les Wexner's mansion.

Do you think Epstein's disdain for Tehran had anything to do with Trump's decision to bomb Iran?

Probably not. But it's notable that Donald's "military excursion" is something his old pal Jeff Epstein would likely have approved of—and would certainly have figured out multiple ways to profit from.

But we're past 115 pages, so this is a good place to wrap up this chapter.

CHAPTER 5
FOR THE SEXUAL ENJOYMENT OF DEFENDANT TRUMP

"Keaton always said, 'I don't believe in God, but I'm afraid of him.'
Well, I believe in God, and the only thing that scares me is Keyser
Soze."

 —Verbal Kint, *The Usual Suspects*

DID **you do that on purpose?**

Do what?

For the epigraph, you used a movie line spoken by Kevin Spacey—the Hollywood actor most associated with Jeffrey Epstein.

Oh, wow. No, I didn't even realize it. I just wanted a quote that expressed a deep-seated fear that most people can't fully understand.

But while we're on the subject: Spacey was with Epstein exactly once—on the highly publicized humanitarian mission to Africa, in 2002, *with his friend Bill Clinton.*[1]

If you're Kevin Spacey, and your pal who happens to be

an ex-president asks you along for this sort of trip, you don't respond with, "I'd love to go, but I'm not sure about this guy whose plane we're flying on."

Literally no one would do that. You trust that an actual ex-president would not outsource the vetting of Jeffrey Epstein to an actor who merely played a president on Netflix.

Because back then, no one knew who Jeffrey Epstein was.

If they knew *who* he was, they didn't know *what* he was.

Let's keep quoting Verbal Kint: "Nobody ever saw him or knew anybody that ever worked directly for him, but to hear Kobayashi tell it, anybody could have worked for Soze. You never knew. That was his power. The greatest trick the Devil ever pulled was convincing the world he didn't exist."

This is really important to understand: people—not just Spacey, but many other prominent people—trusted that Epstein was kosher *because* he was tight with Clinton and Larry Summers and Bill Gates and John Brockman and the list goes on. Epstein used those reputable men to trust-wash himself.

There are plenty of reasons not to like Kevin Spacey as a person. This is not one of them.

You're stalling again.

You're the one who brought up Kevin Spacey.

Answer the question! Why is Trump so afraid of releasing the Epstein Files?

Right, right. What could be worse than the rapes, the history of sexual assault, the Putin puppetry, the mob ties, the felony conviction, and the long relationship with the world's most notorious child sex traffickers?

As I wrote in Chapter Two:

We already know Trump is a serial sexual assailant. We know he's an adjudicated rapist. We know he's a felon, convicted on 34 counts. We know he's a Kremlin stooge. We know he launders money for the Russian mob. We know he comes from the world of organized crime. We know he's a rat.

We know he was best buddies with Epstein for at least a decade and a half—that he partied with him and shared an interest in underaged girls. We know he allowed Epstein and GMax to "steal"—his word—girls from Mar-a-Lago for them to traffic and rape.

We know all of that already. None of it has moved the needle. *Part of the White House* has fallen, but Trump remains.

We also know that whatever's in the Epstein files is very very *very* bad—worse than any of the stuff we *already* know. That's been trickling out in reporting by David Shuster and Allison Gill, among others.

We know there's a push within the Bureau to disclose what's in those files. We know this because Jason Leopold's FOIA request about the FBI's review and redaction of the Epstein files was cranked out in *record* time; it can take many months, and sometimes years, to get replies to FOIA requests, and many of them bring back little of value. Leopold got this one back in a matter of weeks, and it was enlightening.

Finally, we know that Donald Trump never wants the Epstein files to see the light of day. He's genuinely terrified that what's contained there will end his presidency. Why else would his lickspittle Kash Patel authorize $851,344 in overtime for FBI agents to redact *Donald's name* from the documents?

So the question we have to ask ourselves is, hypothetically speaking, what could possibly be worse—I mean, like, *orders of magnitude* more damning—than what we *already* know? Because what we already know is awful.

And now that the legal deadline for releasing the files has come and gone—A comical number of redactions! A million more files found under the couch cushions! Five million more pages!—it's more obvious than ever that Trump is hiding something very very very very bad.[2]

Like, *he kidnapped the president of Venezuela* to get us to stop talking about Epstein. He *started a war with Iran*! *That's* how bad it is.

Out with it, then! What would be worse than the rapes, the history of sexual assault, the Putin puppetry, the mob ties, the felony conviction, and the long relationship with the world's most notorious child sex traffickers?

[sighs]

Please understand that *this is a thought experiment.* I am not accusing Trump of doing any of these things. I am merely answering your question: what *would* be *objectively* worse—hypothetically speaking! hypothetically!—than the rapes, the history of sexual assault, the Putin puppetry, the mob ties, the felony conviction, and the long relationship with the world's most notorious child sex traffickers.

Like, pretend I'm the new showrunner for this horrible TV show that CBS has extended for another season because Bari Weiss is now also in charge of programming, and we're in the Writers Room with Matt Taibbi and Jack Posobiec, kicking ideas around.

This doesn't even raise to the level of "speculation." This is just brainstorming. That's all it is.

I get it. I'm not a child.

Yeah, but the people running our government are. Have you *seen* the White House Twitter feed?

[*beat*]

I feel like there should be an affidavit—like I should sign something. So I get full immunity here.

Stop stalling, dammit.

Very well. But don't say I didn't warn you.

I won't say you didn't warn me. Now, please. Proceed. What would be worse?

Let's begin with the one we've already heard about: Trump "blowing Bubba."[3]

From: jeffrey E. [mailto:jeevacation@gmail.com]
Sent: Wednesday, March 21, 2018 10:43 AM
To: Mark L. Epstein ███████████████
Subject: Re: hey

you mean DONNI TEE

On Wed, Mar 21, 2018 at 9:54 AM, Mark L. Epstein ███████████████ wrote:
You and your boy Donnie can make a remake of the movie Get Hard.

Sent via tin can and string.

On Mar 21, 2018, at 09:37, jeffrey E. <jeevacation@gmail.com> wrote:

and i thought- I had tsuris

On Wed, Mar 21, 2018 at 4:32 AM, Mark L. Epstein ███████████████ wrote:
Ask him if Putin has the photos of Trump blowing Bubba?

From: jeffrey E. [mailto:jeevacation@gmail.com]
Sent: Monday, March 19, 2018 2:15 PM
To: ███████████████
Subject: Re: hey

All good. Bannon with me

By now, we've all seen the photo of Trump appearing to grab at Clinton's junk:

I ask: How would MAGA react to a clip of their mighty alpha male on his knees with a mouth full of 42?

Oh, dear God.

Hey—you asked for this.

I know, I know.

And what if Clinton then made a public statement confirming it's real? "I *did* have sexual relations with that man, Donald Trump…"

You think…?

No, of course not. Remember: thought experiment. Writers Room.

Also, Clinton's statement, released through his spokesman right before Christmas 2025, demanded that then-Attorney General Pam Bondi release *all* the files relating to Clinton, and accuses the Trump Justice Department, so-called, of "insinuation—using selective releases to imply wrongdoing about individuals who have already been repeatedly cleared by the very same Department of Justice, over many years, under Presidents and Attorneys General of both parties."[4]

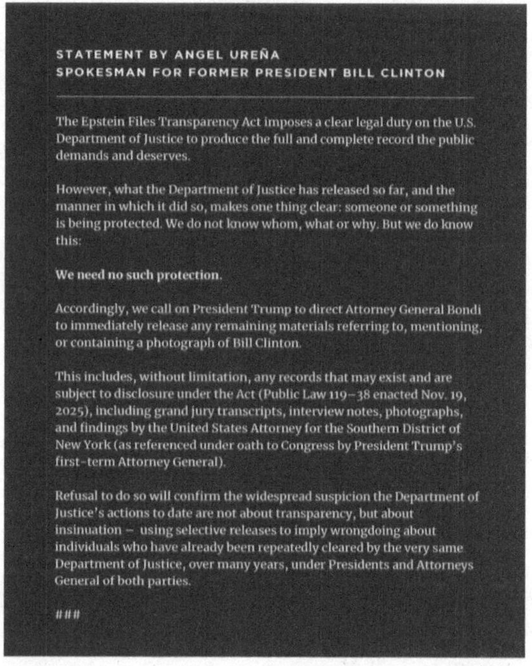

STATEMENT BY ANGEL UREÑA
SPOKESMAN FOR FORMER PRESIDENT BILL CLINTON

The Epstein Files Transparency Act imposes a clear legal duty on the U.S. Department of Justice to produce the full and complete record the public demands and deserves.

However, what the Department of Justice has released so far, and the manner in which it did so, makes one thing clear: someone or something is being protected. We do not know whom, what or why. But we do know this:

We need no such protection.

Accordingly, we call on President Trump to direct Attorney General Bondi to immediately release any remaining materials referring to, mentioning, or containing a photograph of Bill Clinton.

This includes, without limitation, any records that may exist and are subject to disclosure under the Act (Public Law 119–38 enacted Nov. 19, 2025), including grand jury transcripts, interview notes, photographs, and findings by the United States Attorney for the Southern District of New York (as referenced under oath to Congress by President Trump's first-term Attorney General).

Refusal to do so will confirm the widespread suspicion the Department of Justice's actions to date are not about transparency, but about insinuation – using selective releases to imply wrongdoing about individuals who have already been repeatedly cleared by the very same Department of Justice, over many years, under Presidents and Attorneys General of both parties.

###

I highly doubt that "no such protection" and "selective releases" were meant as *doubles entendres*. Although if the "blowing Bubba" bit it true…and Clinton knows there's footage of that…and he then *demands* that the DOJ put it out there? That might be the baller move of the century.

Hmm. What if Bubba were not Bill Clinton, but another man named Bubba?

Or men—plural.

What if Bubba were a boy?

You're catching on.

Or a dog?

Or a horse.

But you don't really think…?

That there's footage of Trump fellating the runner-up of the Belmont Stakes? Of course not. Again: brainstorming. Writers Room.

With that said, "Donald blowing Bubba," where "Bubba" is another man, isn't as far-fetched as it may seem at first blush. There have long been rumors of Trump engaging in sexual activity with Epstein.

Remember, Donald was the protégé of Roy Cohn, the "heterosexual who likes to have sex with men." Cohn liked him because he thought Trump looked like a blonde Elvis. Donald was around Cohn all the time. So it's not like he'd never encountered gay sex before.

Plus, and we don't want to get into stereotypes here, but, I mean—he's a fastidious dresser, fussy about his hair, wears a lot of makeup and (per Noel Casler) a girdle and a ladies' watch (you can clock the watch in that photo with Clinton).

He's obsessed with interior design. He hates women, loves showtunes, and his greatest dream is to build a big beautiful ballroom. His theme song is "YMCA"! He was friends with Liberace![5]

Bullshit.

He was. Seriously. Liberace stayed at Trump Tower during his 1985 Radio City Musical Hall run.[6] Michael Jackson—another Epstein associate—was their mutual friend. MJ even stayed in Liberace's guest bedroom at Trump Tower for a few weeks, when he was in town recording.

Dude, I think you broke my brain.

[beat]

What is it?

I was just thinking about how, when Roy Cohn was dying of what he never admitted was complications due to HIV, Trump cut him out of his life completely. Wouldn't go see him. Abandoned him. Ghosted him.

And?

He apparently did the same thing with Epstein. It's sad. Those may well have been the two most important men in his life.

[pause]

Other than Bubba, of course.

You know, I'm not sure people would care if Trump was gay, or bi, or that he blew Bubba.

People *shouldn't* care. More importantly, a man having consensual sexual relations with another man is not illegal, let alone objectively worse than…whatever Donald did with Jeffrey Epstein.

But if Trump was Bubba's *bottom*, MAGA would care. And if there were boys involved, MAGA would *definitely* care. These are the same maniacs who almost shot up Comet Ping Pong because they thought it was the nexus of Hillary Clinton's secret child sex trafficking operation.

True.

Hey, for all we know, Nicholas Maduro is Bubba.

That's a joke, right?

I think so?

But let's move into a far more likely possibility—Donald raping minors procured for him by his dear friends Jeffrey and Ghislaine.

Wait just a minute! The *New York Times* story says there have been no accusations involving Trump.

The same paper that dismissed Epstein's obvious ties to various intelligence agencies as "conspiracy theories?"[7] *That New York Times*? The one whose publisher's name was among those on the list Epstein made for "Bannon Steve?" The one that employs Epstein apologist and serial bore David Brooks?

We're talking about the same newspaper, yeah? The one that the editor they interview in the new Seymour Hersh documentary says—and I'm paraphrasing—"hates to be beaten but is very uncomfortable being first on a story, particularly one critical of the government?" *That* newspaper? The one I call the *NYeT*?

I guess?

Here's the relevant paragraph:[8]

> Over the years, Mr. Epstein or his partner, Ghislaine Maxwell, introduced at least six women who have accused them of grooming or abuse to Mr. Trump, according to interviews, court testimony and other records. One was a minor at the time. None have accused Mr. Trump himself of inappropriate behavior.

That's simply not true—unless the *Times* considers tying a 13-year-old girl to a bed and violently raping her to *not* be inappropriate.

That's what was alleged in two lawsuits against both

Trump and Epstein: one filed in California on April 26, 2016, under the name Katie Johnson[9]; the second filed in the Southern District of New York on June 20, 2016, under the name Jane Doe. It's the same woman filing both lawsuits.[10]

So: trigger warning.

At the time of the alleged rapes, Katie/Jane was 13 years old. Another alleged victim, "Maria Doe," was just 12. Epstein and Trump were (allegedly) well aware of how young they both were. ("May every day be another wonderful secret.") She knew they knew because, as she explains in a video taken by her attorney (see below), Trump kept telling her, lecherously, that she reminded him of his daughter.

Katie/Jane was brought to Epstein's stately New York residence—known then as "the Wexner mansion," incidentally—by a woman named Tiffany, whose declaration is included in the second lawsuit and corroborates the allegations.[11]

On four separate occasions, Trump allegedly sexually abused Katie/Jane—with the violence and depravity escalating with each encounter. The first time, she gave him a handjob; the second time, oral sex. The last two incidents are detailed in the California lawsuit:

On the third occasion involving the Defendant, Donald J. Trump, the Plaintiff, Katie Johnson was forced to engage in an unnatural lesbian sex act with her fellow minor and sex slave, Maria Doe, age 12, for the sexual enjoyment of Defendant Trump. After this sex act, both minors were forced to orally copulate Defendant Trump by placing their mouths simultaneously on his erect penis until he achieved sexual orgasm. After zipping up his pants, Defendant Trump physically pushed both minors away while angrily berating them for the "poor" quality of their sexual performance....

On the fourth and final sexual encounter with the Defendant, Donald J. Trump, the Plaintiff, Katie Johnson, was tied to a bed by Defendant Trump who then proceeded to forcibly rape Plaintiff Johnson. During the course of this savage sexual attack, Plaintiff Johnson loudly pleaded with Defendant Trump to "please wear a condom". Defendant Trump responded by violently striking Plaintiff Johnson in the face with his open hand and screaming that "he would do whatever he wanted" as he refused to wear protection. After achieving sexual orgasm, the Defendant, Donald J. Trump put his suit back on and when the Plaintiff, Katie Johnson, in tears asked Defendant Trump what would happen if he had impregnated her, Defendant Trump grabbed his wallet and threw some money at her and screamed that she should use the money "to get a fucking abortion".

Further details can be found in the first declaration attached to the New York lawsuit:[12]

Immediately following this [final] rape, Defendant Trump threatened me that, were I ever to reveal any of the details of Defendant Trump's sexual and physical abuse of me, my family and I would be physically harmed if not killed.

Immediately following [Epstein's] rape, just like Defendant Trump, Defendant Epstein threatened me not to ever reveal any of the details of Defendant Epstein's sexual and physical abuse of me or else my family and I would be physically harmed if not killed….

Both Defendants had let me know that each was a very wealthy, powerful man and indicated that they had the power, ability and means to carry out their threats. Indeed, Defendant Trump stated that I shouldn't ever say anything if I didn't want to disappear like Maria, a 12-year-old female that was forced to be involved in the third incident with Defendant Trump and that I had not seen since that third incident, and that he was capable of having my whole family killed.

Tiffany Doe, Epstein's "party planner" and recruiter, who was in her mid 20s at the time of the alleged rapes, was a witness to *all* of this:[13]

> I personally witnessed four sexual encounters that the Plaintiff [Katie/Jane] was forced to have with Mr. Trump during this period, including the fourth of these encounters where Mr. Trump forcibly raped her despite her pleas to stop....
>
> I personally witnessed the one occasion where Mr. Trump forced the Plaintiff and a 12-year-old female named Maria perform oral sex on Mr. Trump and witnessed his physical abuse of both minors when they finished the act....
>
> I personally witnessed Defendant Trump telling the Plaintiff that she shouldn't ever say anything if she didn't want to disappear like the 12-year-old female Maria, and that he was capable of having her whole family killed.

If you'd rather watch and listen than read, there's a video of Katie/Jane detailing the allegations.

Note that this was recorded in February of 2016—before Epstein was a household name, before the Russian stuff started to come out, before the *Access Hollywood* tape, before Trump even won the primary. Back then, most people assumed Donald Trump was no different than the guy that Putin-fluffing traitor Mark Burnett presented to us on *The Apprentice*.

At 17:00, Katie/Jane says:

> The fact that Trump has a chance to be the next president makes me feel disgusting inside. I've always been proud to be an American. I think we live in a beautiful country. But I just see him ruining everything. He's a horrible—what he portrays in the outside isn't even that great, but people don't even know the half of how evil, how sick and twisted that man is.

· · ·

Welp, she sure got *that* right.

A prophetess, she is.

In the video, Katie/Jane recalls a scene Trump had her and Maria act out—a sexual fantasy he wanted them to indulge in. In Trump's fantasy, the two girls are his maids, and he walks in on them making out. So the two girls did as they were told.

But Donald, she says, got all weird, and directed racial epithets at Maria, who was Latina. He *threatened to call INS on her and have her deported*. Which is, of course, what Trump had his *Obergruppenführers* Stephen Miller and Kristi Noem, and that perjuring little shit Greg Bovino, doing to Latino Americans all across the country.

If Katie/Jane's allegations are true, then ICE is Trump's sexual fantasy writ large. He *literally* gets off on what they're doing.

Again, Katie/Jane gave this testimony in *February 2016*—over *ten full years ago*.

Also: *these rapes allegedly happened at Epstein's house*—the one we know was wired up with surveillance equipment. We think, what, Captain Kompromat wasn't using those cameras on the regular?

Why was this not given more attention by the media?

Like who? The poltroons at the *New York Times*?

But, to answer more specifically: because the lawsuits were subsequently withdrawn, ostensibly out of fear for Katie/Jane's physical safety.

It's also possible that Trump paid her off. We don't know.

The reprehensible way our society treats the other survivors likely did not inspire much confidence that she would be protected from the wrath of a desperate criminal who is quite literally the most powerful man in the world.

Plus, Kash Patel is running the FBI now. He makes J. Edgar Hoover look like Atticus Finch.

Kash Patel is the titular Director of the FBI. He ain't running shit—except for his mendacious mouth at Congressional hearings.

Ouch!

And now the *Times* forgets that Katie/Jane exists.

Here's the thing: Just because the lawsuits were withdrawn doesn't make the accusations false.

You think Katie/Jane is telling the truth?

Why would she make that up? And why would attorneys, who only get paid if they win the case, take her on as a client? Twice?

Put it this way: I don't see Trump suing her for defamation.

Is there anything corroborating her allegations in the files?

Yes. In one of the documents the DOJ released by mistake, took back, redacted, and re-released, it talks about Trump having sex with a girl whose "pert nipples" he got off on sucking until they were raw:

several girls at any one time. She confided in me about her casual "friendship" with Donald. Mr Trump definitely seemed to have a thing for her and she told me how he kept going on about how he liked her "pert nipples".

Donald Trump liked flicking and sucking her nipples until they were raw. One evening when we were showering together she showed me her nipples. They looked incredibly painful as they were red and swollen and I remember wincing when I looked at them. I also know she had sexual relations with Trump at Jeffery's NY mansion on regular occasions as I once met Jen for coffee, just before she was going to meet Trump and Epstein together at his mansion.

I will shortly start forwarding you, all the emails which I have managed to save. They include the following:

I moved from Edinburgh to New York in September 2006, where shortly after I was introduced to Jeffery Epstein by Natalie.

. A couple months later, after he constantly stalked me around Edinburgh, I moved to New York to get as far away from him as possible and to start a new life.

I will send you that photo, amongst others as soon as I am able to fly back to the UK next week as I definitely, 100% have it all in my little storage box. I also have other photo's of the Epstein girls and I, whilst on the Island including a couple of pictures of me with Sergey Brin and his then finance Anne Wojcicki. I met the pair when they visited the Island for the day as Sergey wanted try out his new kite surfing equipment as he had only just started kite surfing and was very eager to try out his new equipment with us girls.

 In my secret box, I also have old sim cards which still contain old text messages and telephone numbers which I will have to send you next week once I have them. Hopefully Jens number will be there and I can trace her somehow, surely?

* Email exchanges with Sarah Kellen which includes flight tickets booked for me to St Thomas.

*Email exchanges with Lesley Groff ,which proves that I was asked to source girls from modelling agencies when I went home to see my family in Cape Town. How Jeffery used education as a way for me to trade my soul to the Devil and become a sex slave to pay for my studies at FIT in New York.

 I was desperate to get qualified and get a proper career. The email also show's evidence that I had to become almost anorexic for Jeffery to even entertain the idea of him paying for my tuition. As you will see, Lesley Groff asked me to send her a picture for Jeffery.

I would like to point out that I had to regularly send nude photo's to Lesley so that Jeffery could check how my body looked and if I was putting on any weight.

* An email which was exchanged between   using his code name   via Sugar Daddie.com. I have other correspondence which I had with him in my storage box England.

* Email exchanges between the girl Natalie Malyshev whom received funds from Jeffery for

Although apparently this is an old document, originally released during the Biden years.

. . .

Who is Natalie Malyshev?

Natalya is her given first name. She's one of Epstein's alleged "recruiters," and a party to a lawsuit by Jane Doe 43, along with Epstein, GMax, Sarah Keller, and Lesley Groff. It's CASE NO.: 1:17-CV-00616 in the Southern District of New York.

The new document is, I believe, part of Jane Doe 43's lawsuit. And Jane Doe 43 is NOT Katie/Jane.

So…

Pace the venerable and oh-so-esteemed *New York Times*, we have more than one allegation by an Epstein survivor against Donald Trump.

Why is the legacy media so slow to connect the dots?

Please. They won't even call a lie a lie—*still*, in twenty-fucking-twenty-six.

We're running out of vowels to buy before we have to solve the puzzle—although the legacy media, almost exclusively owned and operated by his oligarch buddies, will continue to play dumb.

So you think the legacy media is…

Complicit. The word you're looking for is *complicit*. Yes. Not the individual reporters, mind you—even at the *NYeT*, there are plenty of really good journalists doing really important work.

But the oligarchs that own the legacy media and the social media? Elon Musk and Zuck, Jeff Bezos and Rupert Murdoch? At this point, the ignorance can't be written off as incompetence.

• • •

So it's intentional?

It certainly appears that way. Almost like all the bloated plutocrats who lined up behind Trump at his second inaugural have a vested interest in keeping him in the White House or something.

We're getting off track again.

Sorry.

Bottom line: It's not difficult to picture Trump, with his long history of sexual assault, yen for young girls, and propensity for violence, doing *exactly* what is alleged in that lawsuit.

Now—what if what Katie/Jane says really happened, and *there's footage in the Epstein files* of that rape scene, or the scene involving her and Maria, or both?

Yeah, that would be worse than what we know.

It would.

So would incest.

Wait—what?

I'm not going to spell this out. Use your imagination.

It's not difficult to put two and two together here; there's lots of examples, in public videos we've already seen, of Donald articulating his lustful desires for Ivanka.[14]

When Katie/Jane alleged that Donald told her she reminded him of his daughter, it didn't make him want to take her out for ice cream.

Jesus Christ.

Keep the Prince of Peace out of this!

Besides, you have to go back farther than the Gospels to find the relevant Bible passage. Leviticus 18, which forbids incest, doesn't explicitly prohibit father-daughter fucking—as I'm sure Paula White and the other Evangelicals who fawn over Trump well know.[15]

Might Epstein's files contain video proof?

I hate to ask but…what's worse than incest?

Snuff.

The ex-GOP political strategist Cheri Jacobus has long speculated that there is a Trump snuff film.[16]

Pardon my ignorance, but…what's a snuff film?

A video of someone being killed.

I had to ask.

What if there were video evidence of Donald Trump violently *murdering* the 12-year-old Maria, whom he allegedly told Katie/Jane had "disappeared?" What if there's *more than one* snuff film?

Wait—isn't there an allegation in the latest tranche about Trump and Epstein throwing a newborn baby into Lake Michigan?

There is—and in that telling, Donald is the dead baby's daddy. Personally, I think that's bullshit—although with Trump, no atrocity would *completely* surprise me.

Remember, some of the material in the files is stuff that isn't true.

· · ·

Like the fake postcard from Epstein to Larry Nassar?

Like the fake postcard from Epstein to Larry Nassar.[17]

Then why release it at all?

In the hopes that the media, which generally operates like cats with a laser pointer, will run with the easily disprovable Lake Michigan story, which, when it turns out to be "fake news," would make every *subsequent* story seem like "fake news."

That and to desensitize us for what's coming.

What's coming?

What if the reason there have been so few Epstein survivors publicly accusing Trump is because *none of them lived to tell the tale?*

Oh my *God* is that dark. Is that even a possibility? It can't be.

Brainstorming! Writers Room! Remember, all I'm trying to do is suggest things that *would be*, in a vacuum, worse. Things that would end not only his presidency, but his freedom.

Murder of a child *would* do it.

Are we sure about that?

One would like to imagine that, despite his boasts to the contrary, if Trump did in fact shoot a man on Fifth Avenue, he would not get away with it.

Dude, you've got a twisted imagination.

Look, *I'm* not the mobbed-up Kremlin-owned elected official who's scared shitless about being exposed for what he did with his buddy the child-sex-trafficking pedophile. I'd rather not think about this stuff at all, believe me.

Besides, there are possibilities that *don't* involve rape and incest and murder. Namely: money, election fuckery, treason, contagion, terrorism.

Well, we can rule out election fuckery. Epstein was dead by 2020.

Not twenty *twenty*; twenty *sixteen*.

I don't follow.

We already know that election was fishy. The Russians interfered. Volume 5 of the Senate Intelligence Committee's Report says as much.

Paul Manafort, the chair of Trump's campaign, shared polling data with a Russian intelligence operative *who specializes in election fuckery*. Jared Kushner proposed a backchannel to Moscow via the Russian embassy and met with the president of a sanctioned bank. Torshin and Butina infiltrated the NRA. There was the Trump Tower meeting. And then Donald himself more or less copped to all of it by calling it "the Russian hoax."

I wrote a book about Trump/Russia in 2018, you may recall: *Dirty Rubles*.

You did. It has 217 ratings on Amazon. Four point five stars.

Indeed it does. Thanks to everyone who left a review!

Well, what if Trump really *was* a Manchurian candidate? I'm talking a deliberate, intentional op. What if it wasn't ever about Hillary losing, as we've been told, but *always* about Donald winning—so he could begin the dismantling of

Russia's greatest adversary? What if Trump is even more of a Putin puppet than even *I* thought?

And what if Epstein helped facilitate the election scheme —and there was proof in the files? That would explain why he seemed so miffed, in his dealings with Steve Bannon, after Trump took the White House in 2017. It would also explain Mark Epstein's implication, in the "Bubba" email, that Bannon knows what Putin has on Trump.

Well, among other things, that would make Trump's presidency illegitimate.

Thus invalidating all his pardons—*and* his Supreme Court picks. Which would explain why the Leonard Leo crew have remained in his corner, *and* why the Republicans on the Hill are so reluctant to release the files. Maybe they don't care about Trump as much as they want to make sure their radical Catholic fascists stay on the bench.

Speaking of the Supreme Court—what if the Epstein cover-up isn't about protecting Trump at all, but rather one, or more than one, of the six Justices in Donald's pocket? He needs all six of them, remember, to continue to grant him authoritarian power.

Huh. That would explain why Roberts, Thomas, Alito, Gorsuch, Kavanaugh, and ACB *keep* continuing to grant him authoritarian power.

It sure would.

But, as devoutly as I wish that that smug motherfucker John Roberts turns up in the Epstein files, I don't think he's a pedo. I think he's just a garden-variety fascist white supremacist asshole.

. . .

How about the money? You mentioned the money. We should probably follow the money.

Right, because Mueller wasn't allowed to.

Well, we know there were over a billion dollars in suspicious transactions on Epstein's accounts with JPMorgan Chase. We know the bank didn't disclose this until 2019. We know Trump was significantly in debt to Deutsche Bank when he took office in 2017.[18] We know that, per the Steele Dossier, Trump was rumored to have been promised the commission on the sale of 19 percent of Rosneft—a sale that actually took place.[19] And we know his son-in-law was also underwater on the office building at 666 Fifth Avenue that the Kushner Company unwisely purchased in 2007, right before the real estate market collapsed.

What if there's evidence that the actual creditor was not Deutsche Bank at all, but the sanctioned Vnesheconombank (VEB)—the Russian bank known as Putin's "slush fund?" And what if that loan was forgiven once Trump won the election? What if *that's* why the head of VEB, Sergei Gorkov, met secretly with Kushner during the 2016 transition?[20] What if *this* is what Putin has on Donald (and Jared)? And what if Epstein, who built his career on moving vast sums of money around secretly, facilitated the operation?

You've seen *The Sopranos*. You know what happens when a guy is in debt to the mob up to his eyeballs. There's nothing he won't do.

I'm not sure that's worse, though. Treason, you also said. A broad term. What do you mean by that?

Leading a violent insurrection in which people died isn't enough for you? We're just gonna memory-hole J6, huh?

. . .

MAGA doesn't care about J6. They all think the insurrectionists are heroes. Including that deranged banshee Ashli Babbit.

Okay, what about putting troops in harm's way to benefit Putin? Or Bibi, or MBS, or Xi? Or some lesser foreign punk, like Orbán or Erdoğan?

Selling classified intelligence—which *we already know* he stole when he left the White House? Giving nuclear secrets to our enemies? (In December, Trump's media company merged with TAE Technologies, a company that deals in plasma fusion—nuclear stuff.)[21] Jack Smith seems pretty convinced Trump did something really horrible with the top secret material he stole.

Plus whatever happened at Helsinki. I mean, John O. Brennan said that Helsinki was tantamount to treason. I don't think he was speaking out of turn.

Wait, who is Brennan again?

Oh, nobody who would know anything—just the former head of the Central Intelligence Agency. And a guy Trump has been trying desperately to discredit for years now, for reasons that have never been made clear.

Would that sway MAGA? The treason, I mean?

Probably not. For all their blather about America First, MAGA cares little about national security. Donald has *already* surrendered our foreign policy to the Kremlin, and our global soft power to China, and the Strait of Hormuz to fucking *Iran*, and it's crickets on that side of the aisle.

A lot of the MAGA demographic is old white guys who grew up worshipping Reagan and hating Commies. Why are they now supporting the Kremlin?

I think Trump/Russia is too "high concept" for your average FoxNews zombie to wrap his—it's usually a "his"—feeble mind around.

Also, people hate to be wrong, and to have been made fools of. So rather than issue a *mea culpa*, they double down and pretend that Trump rolling out the red carpet for Putin in Alaska was a show of American strength.

That leaves us with two more of your suggested possibilities. "Contagion," you said. What's that?

You know how MAGA bends over backwards to get everyone to think covid-19 started with a lab leak in Wuhan?

I guess?

During the pandemic, there was a dot-gov website where you could go to order free tests: covidtests.gov. This is what you see when you go there now...a little Easter egg for the hard-core conspiracy nuts:

Then you scroll down and there's all this anti-Fauci stuff. And this:

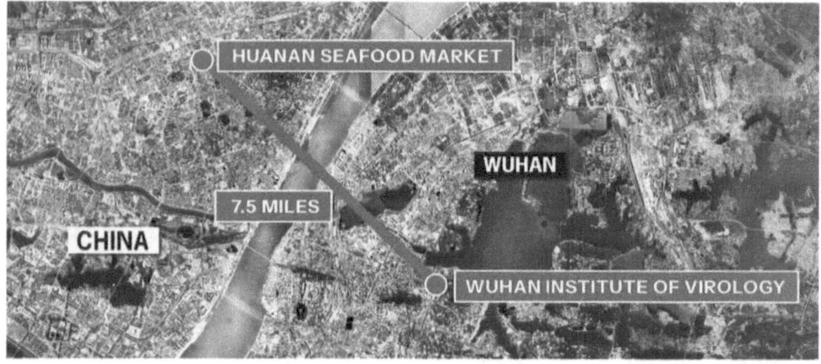

What the...?

I know. Weird, right?

The only actually decent thing Trump ever did as our 45th president was Operation Warp Speed, which helped expedite research and rollout of the covid vaccine.

Donald brags about *everything*. He was excited to get a

"peace prize" invented by a corrupt soccer league, ffs! Why is he running away from his only genuine accomplishment?

Wait—you think Trump had something to do with kickstarting the pandemic?

I'm going to remind you yet again—*we are just brainstorming here.*

No, of course I don't think that. Most likely, the weird website content is him continuing to sully the reputation of Dr. Fauci, to rile up the uneducated he loves so well.

But if Trump insists that the coronavirus was the result of a lab leak, intentional or otherwise…

…then we can safely say the "lab leak" conspiracy theory is bullshit.

Exactly.

And yet he continues to hammer it. Why?

Well, what if the truth was something truly horrifying—and had Trump's tiny fingerprints all over it? What if covid-19 originated not in Wuhan, but here in the United States? And what if Donald not only knew, but was somehow responsible?

Seventy million people have gotten covid, worldwide. Over *seven million* have died of it. That's not Stalin body-count numbers, but it's in the Hitler neighborhood.

Holy shit!

Let me re-re-reiterate: *I do not believe this.* I think Fauci's assessment is the correct one. Remember, I'm only writing about this to suggest things in the Epstein files that could be worse than what we already know.

•   •   •

Well, *that* would be worse.

Exactly. So much so that there's only one thing I can think of that would be objectively worse than all of that—no *ifs, ands* or *buts* about it.

Terrorism?

Yes.

Specifically: 9/11.

9/11? What do you mean?

[sigh]

Let me repeat, for the fifty-eighth time: *I am just throwing ideas out there to answer the "what could be worse" question.* I'm not accusing, I'm not reporting, I'm not even speculating. I'm brainstorming. That's all.

Yes, *we know*. Showrunner, Writers Room, Bari Weiss, CBS. You said it a thousand times.

And I'm going to keep saying it.

You said it. Do go on.

If, hypothetically, Epstein and Trump had something to do with Bin Laden, some association that has yet to be disclosed…and if that association revealed advanced knowledge of the attacks, complicity in the planning of the attacks, or both…

Oh, *fuck*. That would *absolutely* be worse.

Exactly.

• • •

But how—hypothetically—would Trump and Epstein be connected to Bin Laden?

As I mentioned in Chapter One, according to the book *Robert Maxwell: Israel's Superspy*, Semion Mogilevich, the head of the Russian mob and Robert Maxwell's business partner, sold a stolen copy of the PROMIS software to Osama Bin Laden. Twenty years later, Bin Laden was located by U.S. law enforcement with help from Felix Sater—a federal Confidential Informant and a guy who once had Trump Org business cards—who leveraged his contacts with the Russian *mafiya* to track UBL down. That implies an *active* connection between al-Qaeda and the Bratva.

Why would Mogilevich want 9/11 to happen?

As Balzac wrote, "Behind every great fortune there is a crime."

You know who gained absolutely nothing from 9/11? Osama Bin Laden. It didn't help his cause, it didn't help his beef with the Saudi royals, it didn't help him personally. It made all of that worse, in fact. And it ended with him being gunned down like a rabid dog in some hovel in Pakistan.

Mogilevich, on the other hand? After 9/11, the lion's share of the FBI's resources were diverted from investigating transnational organized crime—that is, the Russian mob—to "counterterrorism"—that is, a dozen guys in caves in Afghanistan. *No one* benefitted more from the attacks than the Russians.

So Mogilevich did 9/11?

Don't put words in my mouth, Alex Jones.

To be clear: 9/11 happened exactly how the 9/11 Commission said it happened. Islamic terrorists hijacking airplanes. Bin Laden's material support and planning. All of that.

With that said, those two things—that is, 1) Al-Qaeda planning and carrying out the acts of terrorism, and 2) the Russian mob helping out somehow—are not mutually exclusive. Because: how else would Mogilevich have known where Bin Laden was hiding?

Dude.

Furthermore: if there *were* some connection, and Bin Laden knew about that connection, then *ratting Osama out also helped the Russians!* No more worries about a captured terrorist spilling the beans. Instead of sending Sergei and Ivan to Abbottabad, they Jedi-mind-tricked Seal Team Six to do the wetwork for them.

Again—hypothetically.

And if Mogilevich knew where Bin Laden was holed up...
...so did Putin.

Putin has long had an uneasy relationship with terrorism in general and 9/11 specifically. I wrote about it six years ago:

Early in his reign, Putin was keen to remove the Taliban in Afghanistan. The Taliban had put a stop to opium cultivation, which disrupted the heroin business for Semion Mogilevich and the Russian mob, Putin's allies in his new government. Also, the Taliban was not down with the pipeline project, which the legitimate Russian economy needed. He pressured outgoing president Bill Clinton to move on them in 2000, to no avail.

In late June 2001, an Indian magazine reported that a joint force was being planned, with Russian, US, and Indian forces combining to oust the Taliban.

In July 2001, at the Slovenian Summit where he met face to face with Putin for the first time, new president George W.

Bush "looked the man in the eye...found him very straight-forward and trustworthy...[and] was able to get a sense of his soul." I happen to think Bush is savvier than popular reports about him indicate, but even so, *Putin* manipulating *him* is like the Viscount de Valmont seducing Cécile de Volanges....Putin is a master manipulator, willing and able to convey whatever he wants to convey while never backing down on his commitment to defeating the United States; he showed Bush only what he wanted Bush to see.

A Fox News dispatch from 2002 reported that in August 2001, Putin had warned the Bush government of a plot involving suicidal hijackers planning to attack the U.S. This was likely a case of Putin spinning the story after the fact, but it's not beyond the realm of possibility that he had some inkling of what was going down. Our intelligence services heard chatter, after all, which Bush famously ignored.

Putin managed to be the first world leader to call the president after the 9/11 attacks—pledging his total support, of course.

On 12 September 2001, a Russian newspaper claimed that Russian intelligence knew who was behind the attacks and who had implemented them, and that Putin had warned Bush a few weeks in advance. Again, this might have been nothing more than propaganda, portraying the new Russian leader as powerful and in the know, in stark contrast to the reeling Americans.

The birthday of Felix Dzerzhinsky—founder of the Cheka, and Putin's hero—was September 11. This is probably a coincidence, although Russians, like American neo-Nazis, do enjoy this kind of symbolism.

Another Felix, Felix Sater, Donald John Trump's erstwhile business partner, was a Confidential Informant for the FBI, and a good one: he helped the U.S. government track down Osama bin Laden. How would a guy known for solid Russian mob contacts be able to find UBL, presumably an enemy of the Russians? Further, if the Russians knew where bin Laden was hiding, why did Putin not just relay that intel to Bush or Obama directly, since he was so eager to offer his support? Is there any reality in which *Felix Sater* knew where bin Laden was holed up, but spymaster extraordinaire Putin did not?

In a 2018 *New York Times* piece about Bruce Ohr, one of the FBI's top Russian mob experts, Ohr's longtime deputy had this to say: "Until 9/11, organized crime was one of the main priority criminal programs at the Justice Department. Russian organized crime was a focus. Bruce knew a lot of the Russia stuff and traveled there."[22] In other words, 9/11 had the net result of taking the FBI's focus *away* from the Russian mob. This means that the primary beneficiary of the worst terrorist attack on US soil was not Osama bin Laden or the forces of "radical Islam," but rather the despotic leader of the same country that has been our greatest enemy since 1945—as well as his ruthless partners in the criminal underworld. In other words, the guy who came to power by covertly blowing up a few Moscow apartment buildings also benefited enormously when the towers fell.

You really think Putin knew about 9/11?

Who knows? There's plenty of circumstantial evidence suggesting that he did. And he's an evil, genocidal motherfucker who hates the United States. Although Dubya *did* look into his eyes and see his soul, or whatever. So maybe not? Anyway, it doesn't really matter.

Do we know what Trump was up to on 9/11?

We do, because Donald called into a local news show, as

one does, and gave a nine-and-a-half minute unedited live interview, in which he:

- brags about how the building he owns at 40 Wall Street is, once again, the tallest structure in Lower Manhattan.
- reveals a phone call with his "close friend" Larry Silverstein, the real estate developer who signed a lease on the WTC six weeks before the attacks.
- talks at length about the peculiar structural properties of the Twin Towers.
- expresses doubt that airplanes alone could have felled the buildings, and suggests that there had to have been bombs on the planes for them to have penetrated the exterior steel beams.
- notes that Morgan Stanley lost a lot of office space, and also employees, as did an insurance company he uses—presumably Aon. "Some of those firms," he says, "are just gone."
- recalls the time a structural engineer gave him a tour of the basement of the WTC after the 1993 bombing, demonstrating a deep familiarity with the complex's architecture—including its vulnerabilities.
- seems more put out that the skyline has changed than that so many people died.
- opines that the attacks are "worse than Pearl Harbor."

Wait—is Trump a Truther?

No, no, no.

Nowadays, of course, any deviation from the official explanation is denounced as tin-foil-hat conspiracy theory, on par with chem-trails and fake moon landings. On the actual day of 9/11, however, which is when that video was recorded, most people in New York were saying things similar to what Trump said—including expressing doubt that the planes alone could have felled the buildings.

I was in Manhattan that day, so I speak from experience. Once you were out of harm's way, you were talking about what happened, trying to piece it all together. That's what it was like on the ground.

Nothing that Trump says in that interview suggests prior knowledge. Even the bit about *his* building now being the tallest is not as callous as it might come off today. I remember on 9/11, as I walked past the Empire State Building on my way downtown, noting in my mind that it was once again the tallest structure in the city—and morbidly joking to myself that it had motive.

So Trump had nothing to do with 9/11.

I never said he did! Writers Room, remember? I only said that something involving 9/11 would be worse than what we already know.

Although…

Yes?

Trump keeps bringing it up. He says he "predicted" Bin Laden. Says he wrote about it in his book. Says his book came out a year before the attacks. Says he wrote that Bin Laden was "a bad guy who we have to take out."

Is that claim true?

No. There's no such passage in any of his books. The lone reference to Bin Laden in his 2000 tome, the uncomfortably-titled *The America We Deserve*, concerns the government's alleged habit of manufacturing new enemies:

> Instead of one looming crisis hanging over us, we face a bewildering series of smaller crises, flash points, standoffs, and hot spots. We're not playing the chess game to end all chess games anymore. We're playing tournament chess — one master against many rivals. One day we're all assured that Iraq is under control, the UN inspectors have done their work, everything's fine, not to worry. The next day the bombing begins. One day we're told that a shadowy figure with no fixed address named Osama bin-Laden is public enemy number one, and U.S. jetfighters lay waste to his camp in Afghanistan. He escapes back under some rock, and a few news cycles later it's on to a new enemy and new crisis.

His claim has been thoroughly debunked.[23] It's a lie.

And yet he keeps talking about it. A few months ago, on Air Force One, Lindsey Graham brought up Bin Laden, and Trump launched into this tall tale again, telling the press corps:[24]

> Do you know I wrote about Bin Laden one year before the attack at the World Trade Center, and I said, 'You gotta go after Bin Laden.' It was in my book. Very few people want to say that, but it was in my book…If they would have listened to me, they would have taken out Bin Laden, and you wouldn't have had the World Trade Center tragedy. Did you know that? I predicted Bin Laden.…I wrote a book, it was *one year before the attack* that the book came out…and there's a whole page, a whole section dedicated to—there's a guy named Bin Laden, who's a bad guy, who you have to take out.

What does Trump mean by "very few people want to say that?"

You tell me.

Now, this is almost certainly another one of the braggadocios bullshit narratives that Donald's convinced himself is true. But "I predicted Bin Laden" can also be read as a confession.

A confession to what?

To knowing about the attacks in advance.

Hang on. This is a lot to process. My head is spinning.

Take your time.

So, how would Trump, or Epstein, or anyone, be "involved" with 9/11? Like, how would such an involvement manifest itself?

Foreknowledge.

Foreknowledge would ensure that, if you worked in the World Trade Center—like if you were, say, Howard Lutnick, now the gaslighting Commerce Secretary, then Jeffrey Epstein's next-door neighbor and the CEO of Cantor Fitzgerald, a financial firm with offices on the upper floors of 1 World Trade Center, whose 658 New York-based employees died when the towers fell—you would have found some excuse not to go in that day.

Wait—do you think Lutnick…?

Oh, God, no! Don't get the wrong idea. Remember: I'm not making accusations. I'm not even speculating. I'm just doing hypotheticals. This is a thought experiment—nothing more.

People take days off all the time. And Lutnick didn't even take the *day* off—he went in late because he was taking his son to his first day of kindergarten at Horace Mann.

Also: in terms of weather, September 11, 2001, in NYC was one of the nicest days I can ever remember. It was just *gorgeous* out. So if you were going to pick a day to call out—it would have been a *great* day to do so, for the sunshine alone.

Even now, after months and months of Lutnick blithely lying his ass off for our fascist president, it's hard for me not to admire him because of how he showed up in the aftermath of the attacks.

But Trump didn't work at the World Trade Center.
Correct.

And neither did Epstein.
Also correct.

So how would *they* benefit from foreknowledge?
Mindy Kleinberg, the widow of Alan Kleinberg, a Cantor Fitzgerald employee who died on 9/11, provided this statement to the National Commission on Terrorist Attacks Upon the United States, aka the 9/11 Commission, on March 31, 2003:[25]

On the Chicago Board Options Exchange during the week before September 11th, put options were purchased on American and United Airlines, the two airlines involved in the attacks. The investors who placed these orders were gambling that in the short term the stock prices of both

Airlines would plummet. Never before on the Chicago Exchange were such large amounts of United and American Airlines options traded. These investors netted a profit of at least $5 million after the September 11th attacks.

Interestingly, the names of the investors remain undisclosed and the $5 million remains unclaimed in the Chicago Exchange account.

Why these aberrant trades were not discovered prior to 9/11? Who were the individuals who placed these trades? Have they been investigated? Who was responsible for monitoring these activities? Have those individuals been held responsible for their inaction?

So you think Epstein was the guy who profited from those put options?

In 2004—two years after Kleinberg's statement—the 9/11 Commission released a statement saying that the SEC's investigation

did not develop any evidence suggesting that anyone who had advance knowledge of the September 11 attacks traded on the basis of that information. In the course of our investigation, we examined more than 9.5 million securities transactions that took place during the weeks preceding September 11. Along with the New York Stock Exchange, NASD, the American Stock Exchange, the Chicago Board Options Exchange, the Pacific Exchange, and the Philadelphia Stock Exchange, we reviewed trading in securities and derivative products of 103 companies in six industry groups with trading in seven markets. We also reviewed trading in 32 exchange traded funds and broad and narrow indices. In addition to working with the exchanges and NASD, we worked with criminal law enforcement authorities, including the Department of Justice and the FBI, as well as our regulatory counterparts in the U.S. and abroad. Finally, we sought and obtained information from the legal and compliance departments at securities firms and other financial institutions to determine whether any unusual trading activity had been observed by their staffs in the period prior to Sept. 11, 2001.

So it was just a false rumor?

Well, I mean, this is the same SEC that was, at the time, calling Bernie Madoff to ask for his sage wisdom on regulatory policy, so—grain of salt. But yes, as far as we can tell, it's a false rumor. There were, and still are, a *lot* of false rumors swirling around about 9/11.

The point is, I'm sure that someone as sneaky and smart as Epstein could have figured out ways to make money off the attacks—*if* he had foreknowledge, which, as I keep saying, I don't think he did.

Although if *anyone* did, Epstein did.

How do you mean?

There *was* chatter among various foreign intelligence services that such an attack might be on the horizon. Remember, President Bush himself ignored a Bin Laden warning by the CIA. Epstein was in deep with a lot of foreign intelligence agencies—including Saudi intelligence. It's not inconceivable that he would have had an inkling.

And Trump?

Again: thought experiment. Writers Room.

But…

What if there was evidence in the files that Epstein knew 9/11 was coming, and told his buddy Trump, *just* on the off chance he might be going to the WTC that day—maybe to do another tour of the basement with his structural engineer. And Trump never said anything, never did anything, just hoarded the information for himself—and maybe tried somehow to profit from it?

Like, what if what Mindy Kleinberg alleged was actually true, and there really *were* million-dollar put options on the two airlines the day before 9/11? And what if there was evidence—irrefutable evidence—in the Epstein files that Donald Trump was the guy who, after being informed of the looming attacks, made those purchases?

Jesus.

Or…

Or?

Again: brainstorming. That's all.

As no less an authority than Donald Trump informed us in his rambling 9/11 phone call to the local news station, the Twin Towers had peculiar architectural properties. It follows that the first thing Osama Bin Laden would need, in planning the attacks, were blueprints that *showed* those peculiar architectural properties.

Let's think this through. Bin Laden has no way of getting the blueprints from his Tora Bora redoubt, so he asks his long-time associate Semion Mogilevich for help. Mogilevich in turn asks Epstein. And Epstein goes to his BFF, who is not only familiar with the architectural plans but *has had a structural engineer give him a tour of the WTC basement*—one Donald John Trump.

There are plenty of viable avenues through which Trump

could have scored those blueprints, but I'm not comfortable listing them here, even in a hypothetical scenario. You can figure that part out yourself.

So Trump gives the blueprints to Epstein, who gives them to Mogilevich, who gives them to Bin Laden—thus unknowingly implicating himself in a terrorist attack that, in his own words, was "worse than Pearl Harbor."

In this (again, and I stress: **hypothetical!**) scenario, Trump may not have known what Epstein needed the plans for. But he certainly would have figured it out once the first plane hit the WTC.

Or maybe he *did* know; after all, as he never tires of telling us, he did "predict Bin Laden."

My God.

You ask for a (hypothetical) secret so terrible that Donald would move heaven and earth to keep it under wraps forever? There it is.

I have been thinking about this for months now, and *that* is the single worst thing I can possibly imagine.

You're right. That would be worse. Holy shit.

But for the thousandth time: I'm just answering your question. I'm not accusing, not even speculating. Just brainstorming. That's all. Please don't come at me with Truther bullshit.

I'm too sick to my stomach to come at you with anything.

———

Through death, Jeffrey Epstein escaped justice, escaped reckoning. But what of all his friends and clients? The ones who raped the girls he and Ghislaine trafficked, or else chose to ignore the monstrousness of their comrade? The lawyers, the scientists, the private equity guys, the prince, the governor, the two former presidents—the whole sick crew? They roam free.

What is particularly infuriating about all of this Epstein detective work is how *it shouldn't be necessary.* We shouldn't have to spend our free time looking for a smoking gun in the Epstein Files to "get" Donald Trump. We shouldn't *need* a smoking gun.

The boring, unsexy truth is that, in a just society, *what we already know* about Trump and Epstein is more than enough for the public to universally demand Donald's impeachment, for his own party to turn on him, and for him to spend the rest of his miserable life in social exile, if not in prison.

But ours is not a just society. Not yet.

Not until we collectively decide to make it one.

NOTES

AUTHOR'S NOTE

1. https://gregolear.substack.com/p/the-epstein-files

1. THE MONEY THING

1. Vicky Ward, "What the New Yorker Got Wrong," Vicky Ward Investigates, February 2, 2022
2. Nicole Janok, "Mysterious Man Faces Solicitation Charge," Palm Beach Post, July 24, 2006
3. https://www.finance.senate.gov/imo/media/doc/memorandum_to_senator_wyden_on_jpmc-epstein_redactedpdf.pdf
4. Brooke Harrington, *Offshore: Stealth Wealth and the New Colonialism*, W.W. Norton, 2024.
5. Dipesh Gadher, Home Affairs Correspondent; Gabriel Pogrund, Whitehall Editor; and Tom Pattinson, "How Bullingdon Club links to Jeffrey Epstein in his birthday book," The Sunday Times, September 14, 2025
6. Ibid.
7. Ibid
8. Thomas Hampson, "Part 2: The Troubling Case of Jeffrey Epstein," Illinois Family Institute, July 28, 2025
9. Tom Winter and Rich Schapiro, "Jeffrey Epstein used foreign passport with fake name to enter Saudi Arabia: prosecutors," NBC News, July 17, 2019
10. Thomas Hampson, "Part 2: The Troubling Case of Jeffrey Epstein," Illinois Family Institute, July 28, 2025
11. https://webhelper.brown.edu/cheit/Understanding_the_Iran_Contra_Affair/i-thebeginning.php
12. "Ehud Barak met with Jeffrey Epstein dozens of times, flew on private plane — report," Times of Israel, May 4, 2023
13. Virginia Guiffre, *Nobody's Girl*, 2025
14. Steven Morris, "How 'house of horror' investigation brought Jersey abuse to light," The Guardian, July 3, 2017
15. "Paradise Papers: Queen's private estate invested £10m in offshore funds," BBC, November 6, 2017
16. James Beal, "Jeffrey Epstein sold Prince Andrew's secrets, new book claims," The Sunday Times, August 3, 2025
17. https://www.theguardian.com/news/ng-interactive/2025/oct/25/how-does-he-pay-for-it-all-the-mystery-of-prince-andrews-money

18. https://www.theguardian.com/uk/2010/nov/29/wikileaks-cables-rude-prince-andrew

19. https://www.express.co.uk/news/royal/1324816/royal-family-news-ghislaine-maxwell-robert-maxwell-prince-andrew-princess-diana-spt

20. Gordon Thomas and Martin Dillon, *Robert Maxwell, Israel's Superspy: The Life and Murder of a Media Mogul*, Da Capo Press, 2002.

21. https://www.wexnerfoundation.org/letter-from-les/

22. https://www.reuters.com/article/world/us/jeffrey-epsteins-sexual-abuses-began-by-1985-targeted-13-year-old-lawsuit-cla-idUSKB N1Y72K4/

23. See Hampson, above.

2. COMMODITY FLOW INFORMATION

1. Jesse Kornbluth, "I was a friend of Jeffrey Epstein; here's what I know," Salon, July 9, 2019

2. https://int.nyt.com/data/documenthelper/7061-u-s-v-ghislaine-maxwell-indict/96d918f9d16dbd14e656/optimized/full.pdf

3. Ibid

4. https://www.bbntimes.com/society/meet-scott-gerald-borgerson-ghislaine-maxwell-s-former-husband

5. https://patents.justia.com/patent/12001992

6. http://www.citjourno.org/page-3

7. https://www.buzzfeednews.com/article/anthonycormier/felix-sater-trump-russia-undercover-us-spy

8. https://www.pbs.org/frontlineworld/stories/bribe/2009/04/louis-freeh-interview.html

9. https://docs.house.gov/meetings/JU/JU08/20250227/117951/HHRG-119-JU08-20250227-SD006-U6.pdf

10. https://www.americanfreakshow.news/p/jeffrey-donald-and-melania?utm_campaign=email-half-post&r=2wfp4&utm_source=substack&utm_medium=email

11. https://www.dailymail.com/news/article-7410813/Pictured-Prince-Andrew-partying-Jeffrey-Epstein-Donald-Trump.html

12. Mary Jordan, *The Art of Her Deal: The Untold Story of Melania Trump*, Simon & Schuster, 2020.

13. https://www.americanfreakshow.news/p/jeffrey-donald-and-melania

14. https://www.wilsoncenter.org/publication/312-trafficking-women-after-socialism-to-and-through-eastern-europe

15. https://www.state.gov/semion-mogilevich

16. https://www.americanfreakshow.news/p/the-french-connection

17. https://www.bbc.com/news/world-europe-60443518

18. https://www.factcheck.org/2019/08/baseless-claim-about-barr-visit-to-epstein-prison/

19. Ibid

20. https://www.wexnerfoundation.org/statement-from-les-wexner/

21. https://www.wexnerfoundation.org/letter-from-les/

22. https://www.factcheck.org/2019/08/baseless-claim-about-barr-visit-to-epstein-prison/

23. https://thehill.com/homenews/administration/446491-trump-announces-departure-of-white-house-lawyer-emmet-flood/

24. https://www.nytimes.com/2019/06/01/us/politics/emmet-flood-white-house.html

25. https://journaliststudio.google.com/pinpoint/document-view?collection=092314e384a58618&utm_source=collection_share_link&p=1&docid=764778c7c68fa151_092314e384a58618_0&dapvm=2

26. https://www.bloomberg.com/news/newsletters/2025-11-25/epstein-files-new-fbi-emails-detail-review-special-redaction-project

3. AS IF IN A LABYRINTH

1. https://www.bloomberg.com/news/newsletters/2025-11-25/epstein-files-new-fbi-emails-detail-review-special-redaction-project

2. https://www.thecrimson.com/article/2025/12/12/poetry-show-pulled/

3. https://nymag.com/news/features/41826/

4. Ibid

5. https://nymag.com/news/features/41826/

6. https://www.politico.com/news/magazine/2021/05/14/jeffrey-epstein-investigation-women-487157

7. https://www.wired.com/story/global-girl-jeffrey-epstein-and-the-lolita-express/

8. https://www.independent.co.uk/news/world/americas/nadia-marcinko-jeffrey-epstein-documents-b2475553.html

9. https://resee.it/tweet/1966224661613813813

10. https://www.palmbeachpost.com/story/news/trump/2025/09/03/jeffrey-epstein-case-these-4-women-might-know-about-any-client-list/85937418007/

11. https://www.documentcloud.org/documents/6184602-Jeffrey-Epstein-non-prosecution-agreement.html

12. https://www.washingtonpost.com/technology/2022/03/26/silicon-valley-russia-oligarchs/

13. https://bylinetimes.com/2025/10/20/inside-epsteins-russian-tech-web-how-oligarch-cash-and-three-women-connected-moscow-to-silicon-valley/

14. https://dossier.center/jeffreyepsteinrusconnect-en/

15. https://www.cornellsun.com/article/2025/11/my-boy-jeffrey-is-everywhere-epstein-s-personal-lawyers-reid-weingarten-71-darren-indyke-j-d-91-implicated-in-latest-batch-of-files

16. Ibid

17. https://bocanewsnow.com/wp-content/uploads/2025/12/TRUMP.pdf

18. https://america2.news/part-four-making-sense-of-epsteins-russia-ties/

19. https://www.flickr.com/photos/edyson/9209120/in/photostream/

20. https://dossier.center/jeffreyepsteinrusconnect-en/

21. https://newrepublic.com/article/154826/jeffrey-epsteins-intellectual-enabler
22. Ibid
23. Ibid
24. https://www.bloomberg.com/news/articles/2016-12-22/deutsche-bank-s-reworking-a-big-trump-loan-as-inauguration-nears
25. https://www.ft.com/content/3ed742fd-ee22-475a-92d0-aeb5ce186ad2
26. https://www.telegraph.co.uk/business/2026/02/03/british-fixer-to-elite-made-connections-for-epstein/
27. https://jmail.world/thread/EFTA02006700?view=inbox
28. https://jmail.world/thread/EFTA01861137?view=inbox
29. https://www.lemonde.fr/en/france/article/2026/02/21/documents-show-epstein-s-attempts-at-connecting-with-sarkozy-s-cir cle_6750732_7.html
30. https://www.theguardian.com/business/2025/mar/04/jeffrey-epstein-jes-staley-barclays-ceo-project-jes

4. TOTALLY TRICKED OUT BY UNCLE JEFFREY TODAY!

1. https://amberspeaksup100.substack.com/p/the-island-that-disap peared-from-420
2. https://amberspeaksup100.substack.com/p/zorro-ranch-inside-epsteins-desert
3. https://www.the-sun.com/news/1077692/epstein-zorro-ranch-man ager-vanished/
4. https://alisav.substack.com/p/ghislaine-maxwells-father-sold-bugged
5. Ibid
6. Ibid
7. https://alisav.substack.com/p/epstein-likely-wasnt-the-boss-so?utm_source=post-email-title&publication_id=1790706&post_id=192561831&utm_campaign=email-post-title&isFreemail=false&r=2wfp4&triedRedi rect=true&utm_medium=email
8. https://www.aljazeera.com/news/2026/2/24/how-epstein-tried-to-buy-a-moroccan-palace-months-before-his-death
9. https://jmail.world/thread/vol00009-efta00555661-pdf?view=inbox
10. https://jmail.world/thread/EFTA02313344?view=inbox
11. https://www.justice.gov/epstein/files/DataSet%209/EFTA00526582.pdf
12. https://jmail.world/thread/vol00009-efta00555657-pdf?view=inbox
13. https://www.justice.gov/epstein/files/DataSet%2010/EFTA01266204.pdf
14. https://www.justice.gov/epstein/files/DataSet%209/EFTA00165269.pdf
15. https://kaitjustice.substack.com/p/the-woman-nobody-asks-about-is-the
16. Ibid
17. https://kaitjustice.substack.com/p/stanley-kubrick-filmed-his-warning

18. https://www.justice.gov/age-verify?destination=/epstein/files/Data Set%2011/EFTA02605815.pdf

19. https://www.businessinsider.com/jeffrey-epstein-emails-goldman-sachs-kathryn-ruemmler-attorney-client-privilege-2025-12

20. https://www.washingtonpost.com/politics/aides-despite-denials-knew-of-white-house-tie-to-cartagena-prostitution-scandal/2014/10/08/5b98dc90-4e7e-11e4-aa5e-7153e466a02d_story.html?hpid=z1

21. https://www.justice.gov/epstein/files/DataSet%2011/EFTA02591681.pdf

22. https://www.politico.com/story/2014/10/kathy-ruemmler-attorney-general-withdrawal-112188

23. https://abovethelaw.com/2026/02/ok-we-need-to-talk-about-what-these-kathryn-ruemmler-jeffrey-epstein-emails-really-mean/

24. https://drive.google.com/file/d/1xVzWo7Q8VFFBUsaT5pnDnqMObb KzLUf3/view?usp=sharing

25. https://edition.cnn.com/2023/09/26/business/jpmorgan-jeffrey-epstein-us-virgin-islands

26. https://www.npr.org/2023/06/12/1181675580/epstein-jane-doe-1-290-million-settlement-jpmorgan-chase

27. https://www.barrons.com/articles/jpmorgan-earnings-stock-price-7aa7db98?gaa_at=eafs&gaa_n=AWEtsqeOnevNudwrcNv03UU_gWc V69N-AmBsZeyiN0Pu9ORmozdwYIOdaihWR0iRohk%3D&gaa_ts= 696642d4&gaa_sig=9iSmGO-q29O9ETRZJ_aKqvI8IpKt4NHp9fsAzGpDj JKaSMKI7ZHCFxViw4buSuf0oQsfDA_OFAz4AhhMlP17pw%3D%3D

5. FOR THE SEXUAL ENJOYMENT OF DEFENDANT TRUMP

1. https://www.nytimes.com/2015/02/22/arts/television/kevin-spacey-star-of-house-of-cards-and-a-bromance-with-bill-clinton.html

2. https://www.nbcnews.com/politics/justice-department/justice-depart ment-5-million-pages-jeffrey-epstein-files-trump-rcna251702

3. https://www.fastcompany.com/91443564/epstein-bubba-email-donald-trump-bill-clinton-etsy-merch

4. https://x.com/angelurena/status/2003166064969154839

5. https://medium.com/sexstories/the-curious-tale-of-donald-trump-and-liberace-978d47b512e2

6. https://vocal.media/beat/donald-trump-and-liberace

7. https://www.nytimes.com/2025/12/16/magazine/jeffrey-epstein-money-scams-investigation.html

8. Ibid

9. https://archive.org/stream/jeffrey-epstein-lawsuit-docs-signed/jeffrey-epstein-lawsuit-docs-signed_djvu.txt

10. https://www.courthousenews.com/wp-content/uploads/2024/07/trump-epstein-2016-complaint.pdf

11. https://www.courthousenews.com/wp-content/uploads/2024/07/tiffany-doe-affidavit.pdf

12. https://www.courthousenews.com/wp-content/uploads/2024/07/jane-doe-affidavit.pdf
13. Ibid
14. https://www.yahoo.com/news/no-reason-lets-revisit-trumps-185011716.html
15. https://hermeneutics.stackexchange.com/questions/28759/why-doesnt-leviticus-18-forbid-a-man-from-incest-with-his-daughter
16. https://x.com/CheriJacobus/status/1957112624690204858
17. https://www.theguardian.com/us-news/2025/dec/23/epstein-files-larry-nassar-letter
18. https://www.reuters.com/markets/europe/tired-trump-deutsche-bank-games-ways-sever-ties-with-president-sources-2020-11-03/
19. https://medium.com/@gregolear/rosneft-revisited-did-trump-do-a-deal-in-russia-b2dfda6ce310
20. https://www.nytimes.com/2017/05/29/us/politics/jared-kushner-russia-investigation.html
21. https://www.nytimes.com/2025/12/18/business/trump-media-tae-technologies-fusion-power-deal.html
22. https://www.nytimes.com/2018/08/27/us/politics/bruce-ohr-trump-justice-department.html
23. https://www.factcheck.org/2015/12/trumps-bin-laden-prediction/
24. https://bsky.app/profile/atrupar.com/post/3mbnbxgatlk2h
25. https://govinfo.library.unt.edu/911/hearings/hearing1/witness_kleinberg.htm#:~:text=On%20the%20Chicago%20Board%20Options,of%20both%20Airlines%20would%20plummet.

ABOUT THE AUTHOR

Greg Olear is the *L.A. Times*-bestselling author of three novels and four nonfiction books, including *Dirty Rubles: An Introduction to Trump/Russia* (2018), *Rough Beast: Who Donald Trump Really Is, What He'll Do If Re-Elected, and Why Democracy Must Prevail* (2024), and *The Age of Unreality: Essays on Literature & Tyranny* (2025).

He is the co-host of the weekly live show *The Five 8* and the host of the PREVAIL podcast. His Substack column, PREVAIL, has run on Tuesday, Friday, and Sunday since 2019.

He lives in New York with his family.

For more information, visit gregolear.com.

Photo by Franco Vogt.